W9-BBE-527

Lectures delivered at the 1982 John G. Finch Symposium on Psychology and Religion at the Graduate School of Psychology, Fuller Theological Seminary.

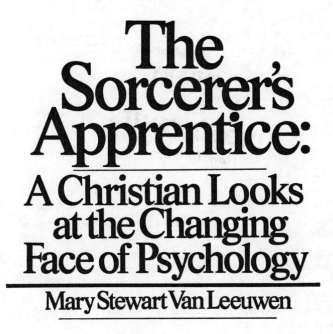

The Sorcerer's Apprentice:

A Christian Looks at the Changing Face of Psychology

Mary Stewart Van Leeuwen

InterVarsity Press
Downers Grove
Illinois 60515

InterVarsity Press is the book-publishing division of Inter-Varsity Christian Fellowship, a student movement active on campus at hundreds of universities, colleges and schools of nursing. For information about local and regional activities, write IVCF, 233 Langdon St., Madison, WI 53703.

Distributed in Canada through InterVarsity Press, 1875 Leslie St., Unit 10, Don Mills, Ontario M3B 2M5, Canada.

All Scripture quotations, unless otherwise indicated, are from the Revised Standard Version of the Bible, copyrighted 1946, 1952, © 1971 and 1973.

ISBN 0-87784-398-8

Printed in the United States of America

Library of Congress Cataloging in Publication Data

Van Leeuwen, Mary Stewart, 1943-
    The sorcerer's apprentice.

    "Lecture delivered at the 1982 John G. Finch
Symposium on Psychology and Religion at the Graduate
School of Psychology, Fuller Theological Seminary"–P.
    Includes bibliographical references and index.
    1. Psychology–Methodology.   2. Psychology–
Methodology–Religious aspects–Christianity.
I. John G. Finch Symposium on Psychology and Religion
(1982: Graduate School of Psychology, Fuller Theological
Seminary)   II. Title.
BF38.5.V36   1982   150'.1   82-21348

ISBN 0-87784-398-8

17   16   15   14   13   12   11   10   9   8   7   6   5   4   3   2   1
95   94   93   92   91   90   89   88   87   86   85   84   83   82

To Anne and Gordon Bland of Yieldingtree Farm, Zambia
James 5:20

PREFACE

Psychology is unusual among the disciplines making up the current intellectual landscape in training its theoreticians and researchers side by side with its applied practitioners and in bestowing the same title on all three. In my experience, this common labeling of very different pursuits results in endless confusion for lay followers of psychology. Consequently, I see my first task as stating as clearly as possible how this book fits into the complex mosaic of my discipline and my second as stating how the concerns of this volume relate to the ongoing challenge of integrating faith with learning. To both tasks I will attempt to do justice by way of some autobiographical reflections on my own development as an academic psychologist who became a professing Christian only near the completion of my doctoral training.

Like many would-be psychologists, I embarked upon my undergraduate major with mainly applied concerns, hoping to have practical training as a counselor or clinician from the earliest stages of my college requirements. Furthermore, like many undergraduate psychology majors, I was at first staggered by the apparent abstraction of my actual course requirements from the practical business of helping people who were hurting. The relevance of statistics, experimental design, animal learning and psychobiology (more essential for entry to any graduate program than the courses in personality, child development, psychopathology or the history of psychology) to what I had thought was psychology seemed at best slight. Yet, as I and my professors soon discovered, I had a knack for understanding and applying in research settings the strongly natural-scientific approach which dominated the discipline. Such were the rewards of success in these endeavors that by the time I was ready for graduate school, I had concluded that the best compromise between my original applied interests and my acquired scientific ones would be a program in experimental social psychology, which systematically explores the individual's thoughts, perceptions, feelings and behaviors as they are influenced by other persons.

Then, as now, the ruling paradigm for social psychology (as for almost all of American psychology, including much clinical work) was largely borrowed from classical physics, whose model of a material, clockwork universe passively at the mercy of discoverable natural forces was transferred to the human subjects (although never, I soon realized, to the investigators) of psychological research. With regard not only to theory but also to method, American psychology had apprenticed itself to a type of science already fast becoming outdated by Niels Bohr's quantum postulate and Heisenberg's principle of indeterminacy: laboratory experiments, with their stress on systematic manipulation of events under what was presumed to be controlled conditions, were seen as the most promising route to universal, transtemporal laws of psychological functioning.

To all of this was added a surprisingly unreflective faith in evolutionary theory which accounted for the excessive emphasis on the continuity of animal and human behavior.

Although intuitively uneasy about all these features of my discipline, I found any opportunity to articulate that discontent blocked by the pervasive indifference (and often outright hostility) of most American psychology to both metaphysical and philosophy of science concerns—a stance whose historical roots I have attempted to trace in chapter one. Furthermore, it was not until the Hound of Heaven had claimed my total allegiance that my vaguely humanistic unease was transformed into an urgent motivation to examine, in a critically Christian framework, not only the results and applications of prevailing social psychological research but also the very assumptions according to which it was conducted. The fruit of that lengthy search was the discovery of a number of theoretical, methodological and ethical contradictions, troubling to still only a minority of psychologists, at the heart of the entire enterprise. I have attempted to spell out the substance of those contradictions in chapter two, in the course of analyzing a case study of the scientific method as traditionally taught and practiced in social psychology.

The third and final chapter broadens these concerns to encompass human psychology as a whole (including, at times, its clinical-counseling applications) and makes some suggestions for reform which include a greater acknowledgment of certain uniquely human properties previously assumed to be operating in psychological investigators but explicitly ignored or denied in their research subjects. I have labeled these properties *reflexivity, meaning* and *wholeness,* and have attempted to articulate both their significance and their hazards to a psychology reformed according to a biblical perspective. Throughout this chapter runs the message that North American psychology is in a state of profound transition and that now, perhaps as never before, Christians in the field have a very clear opportunity to help shape the future of their discipline. This could be their moment to approach human research done by human investigators in a more consistently biblical way than that under which most of them were—and are still being— trained.

In the course of many helpful discussions with colleagues about the material covered in this volume, two reservations frequently recurred. The first was that a Christian critique of psychology should certainly focus on its underlying theories and its eventual applications but not on its natural-scientific epistemology which, short of revealed truth, was often still seen to be the best available route to psychological knowledge, even if no longer immune to historical and personal distortion. It is perhaps on this issue that I differ most from other recent considerations of psychology in Christian perspective, and I hope that I have argued my case persuasively, yet not inflexibly, in chapters two and three. In the second place, that minority of Christian colleagues who essentially agreed with my position sometimes wondered if I was not flogging a dead horse. In the wake of postmodern physics, they asked, is not naive positivism a thing of the past in the social sciences as well? Do they not all acknowledge that metaphysics has a legitimate place in science and that the whole enterprise is radically conditioned by historical, personal, and other paradigmatic forces in a way that makes for a much greater tolerance of pluralism in both theory and method?

It is significant that none of the colleagues who posed such questions were academics or students in psychology itself. Those who are remain only too aware of the scientific culture lag afflicting that discipline, which even today makes only token acknowledgment of the significance of postmodern science for its own conduct. Current historians and philosophers of science, now sensitized to the very human character of the scientific enterprise, look to psychology for help in examining the host of human factors which interact with the doing of science: perceptual set, language considerations, the importance of professional networks, the nature of scientific apprenticeship and the place of defense mechanisms in resistance to paradigm change, to name but a few—yet North American psychology, for the most part, neither wants to undertake the task nor even understands the necessity for it. The venerable Sigmund Koch summarized it well when he observed that

> while this [post-modern] wave of interest has gathered, psychology has stood on the shore, almost untouched by the spray. Those who know the history of modern psychology will find little cause for surprise in this. We are not known for our readiness to be in the wave-front of history. In every period of our history, we have looked to external sources in the scholarly culture—especially natural science and the philosophy of science—for our sense of direction, and typically we have embraced policies long out of date in those very sources. What is unique about our present day relative to the rest of scholarly culture is that each branch of the latter seems to be either working toward, or inviting into existence, a redefinition of knowledge of a sort which must largely depend on psychological modes of analysis. Yet psychology seems hardly cognizant of the challenge implicit in these circumstances. Or of the circumstances.[1]

Although Koch made these observations some twenty years ago, they have a strikingly contemporary ring. Consequently, *The Sorcerer's Apprentice* has been written for Christians and other thoughtful humanists in and interested in psychology who sense that change is long overdue, but who may not have articulated a conceptual or religious framework within which to argue for reform. It is my hope that this book will be of modest help in that undertaking.

Some acknowledgment is certainly needed of the many sources of aid and encouragement which lie behind the finished volume. The major impetus toward its completion came from an invitation to deliver the chapters as lectures in the 1982

John G. Finch Symposium on Psychology and Religion at the Graduate School of Psychology, Fuller Theological Seminary. I am deeply indebted to all the students and faculty at Fuller who attended those lectures and gave valuable critical feedback on them. In particular I would like to thank Professor Clinton McLemore, the coordinator of the lecture series, and the formal respondents to the lectures, professors Hendrika Vande Kemp, Paul G. Hiebert and Geoffrey Bromiley for their criticism of the text and their clarification of several important issues.

I am grateful to my home institution, York University in Toronto, for the sabbatical time to begin and complete a substantial portion of the text. Thanks are also due to my students at York who read and reacted to it in draft form and to various Toronto colleagues who also read and criticized portions of the manuscript, including Paul Marshall, Donna Rietschlin, Irwin Silverman, and to my husband, Raymond Van Leeuwen, who supported the project faithfully despite the pressures of graduate study on him and the demands of a young family on both of us. The final completion of the manuscript was made possible by a visiting fellowship at the Calvin Center for Christian Scholarship, Calvin College, Grand Rapids, Michigan in 1981-82. I am especially thankful for the many hours lavished on the entire manuscript by other members of the Center team that year, David Lyon, Clifton Orlebeke, Mary Vander Goot and Henk Woldring; by our student affiliates, Robert Kamphuis and Catherine Page; and by our secretary and deciphering expert, Nelle Tjapkes. Stephen Evans of Wheaton College, Paul Vitz at New York University and Glenn Weaver at Calvin also made room in their crowded schedules to read and comment on the completed work.

The generous cooperation of all these people in bringing the book to completion has become, for me, a living example of Christian and intellectual fellowship. It remains only to pray that the Christ whose saving initiative originally planted the seed of the book will be honored in its dispersion and use.

CHAPTER 1

THE APPRENTICESHIP UNDERTAKEN

AMONG THE MANY WORKS produced by Goethe, the nineteenth-century German poet, is a ballad entitled *Der Zauberlehrling*, or "The Apprentice Sorcerer." The song tells how a young sorcerer-in-training gets into difficulties when he tries to apply his master's magic. At the turn of the century the French composer Paul Dukas produced a lively orchestral scherzo based on Goethe's ballad, a piece now well known by the title "The Sorcerer's Apprentice."

In the story an older, more experienced sorcerer goes out one day, leaving his young student-in-residence to do the household chores, including the drawing of the day's water supply. Ill inclined to carry the water pails back and forth from the well, the apprentice uses his novice's supply of magic words to turn the household broom into a robot water carrier. As the broom dutifully bounces back and forth with the pails, the apprentice sits back and congratulates himself on his seemingly successful application of his master's craft. But his pleasure is soon cut short by the realization that he is unable to find the right word to stop the broom's single-minded trips to and from the well. His self-satisfaction turns to panic as the broom proceeds to fill the entire house with water; his attempts to destroy the broom by chopping it to bits only result in the materialization of more and more brooms from the pieces, each bouncing doggedly back and forth with more and more pails of water. As he despairs of saving either himself or the house from a watery grave, the sudden reappearance of the sorcerer himself reverses the chaos created by the apprentice's naive misapplication of his master's knowledge.

Psychology as the Sorcerer's Apprentice

This little story supplies a metaphor for the relationship of North American psychology to its adoptive parent and master, the field of the natural sciences. Insecure and self-conscious about its status as an emerging discipline, midnineteenth-century psychology eagerly attached itself to the approach and methods of the natural sciences, reasoning that their almost magical power to predict and control the ways of inanimate objects and nonhuman organisms would also supply a key to the complete understanding and management of human beings.

Psychology's development since then, particularly in North America, has consisted largely in an exalted overconfidence in the apparent success of this natural-science-based approach to human behavior and higher mental processes. To be sure, there were those who right from the beginning doubted and questioned the appropriateness of studying people in the same way that rocks and rats are studied, but they constituted a minority voice which was relegated more and more to the fringes of the expanding academic establishment in psychology. However, more recent decades in psychology have been characterized by a growing sense of self-doubt. The magic techniques of the parent sorcerer, which seemed at first to show so much promise, began to lead us into dilemmas from which we felt helpless to extricate ourselves. The experimental method, with its associated trappings of quantification and manipulation, had become so dominant a tool that many psychologists conceded its use was the only characteristic uniting the diversity of interests in the profession. Indeed, so much was experimental sophistication the badge of competence for psychologists that it seemed to matter little how profound one's theorizing was, provided that one could invent ever-more-ingenious manipulations and measurements of ever-more-restricted phenomena in the laboratory setting. A graduate student's graffito from the 1960s hinted at the growing discontent: "If it's not worth doing, then it's not worth doing rigorously," the anonymous trainee grumbled.

In addition to the growing suspicion that experimentation was too restricted a tool to probe the richness of the human psyche, there was also a vague uneasiness about the ethical compromises which increasingly surrounded its use. For unlike rocks and rats, human research participants (at least the normal, college-aged ones that made up the majority of psychology's research subjects) did not submit passively to experimental manipulations but actively questioned them and reflected upon them. The standard solution to this problem had become the practice of deliberately deceiving participants as to the true nature of the experiment in order to distract, if not fully eliminate, their speculations about it. It was assumed that, thus caught off guard, they would be properly vulnerable to the experimenter's manipulations. Yet as the years passed the entrenchment of such deception as an accepted and even admired aspect of psychological research also began to make some members of the discipline uneasy.

On both counts—the methodological and the ethical—the youthful field of psychology was beginning to ride over some rough ground. Consequently, in 1955 the annual assembly of science apprentices in psychology called upon one of the master sorcerers, physicist Robert Oppenheimer, to explain just what had gone wrong and how it might be righted. His answer was a relief to some, a threat to many and a surprise to all: Psychology, he said, should never have modeled itself so exclusively after the natural sciences in the first place. Human beings, regardless of what they might share with the merely material and merely animal world, are more than merely material and merely animal and should be approached by psychology in terms of their full humanity. In the course of so studying human beings, he continued, psychology would need to look for methods to at least supplement, if not replace, those of the laboratory scientist, however much it had already invested in these methods and however much its self-image had depended on their mastery and application.[1]

A few heard him; most did not—at least, not most of those whose work took place in the psychology departments of the larger and more prestigious North American universities. It is only now, some twenty-five years later, that there is a discernible shift within academic psychology itself toward a serious reconsideration of Oppenheimer's advice. Why it took us so long, as a presumably intelligent academic community, to hearken to the master sorcerer's words is the subject of the rest of this chapter.

A Brief Look at the History of Natural Science

Natural science as practiced today is the distinctive creation of Europe and its colonial offspring of the sixteenth century onward. At the start of this era, higher education was dominated by an outlook known as scholasticism, which regarded the earth as a living mass created by God to be the center of all heavenly activity and for human benefit, although still strongly influenced as well by demonic and magical agencies. This approach to nature was justified by an appeal to the authority of Scripture, as then interpreted, and the authority of earlier Greek philosophy, particularly that of Aristotle. By contrast, a hundred years later this world view had been almost completely eclipsed by one which saw the earth as merely one of many sun-centered planets in a vast, empty space devoid of human or spiritual properties. As such, it was considered incapable of yielding up its secrets in response to an appeal to mystical insight or inspired authority; rather, the earth and its contents had to be studied soberly, painstakingly and impersonally with the aid only of human sense experience and reason.

Natural science as the servant of technology. Many reasons have been suggested for this eclipse of scholasticism by what has come to be known as the scientific revolution.[2] Certainly one reason was an understandable resentment of antiscientific pressures from the church, which was itself in a state of uncertainty and disorganization, fearful that the reorganization of the universe along the lines advocated by Galileo would lead to the destruction of religious faith and ecclesiastical authority. A second reason regularly cited was the influence of the fifteenth-century Renaissance, an intellectual and artistic movement in which the rediscovery of classical Roman and Greek texts in many fields resulted in a new respect for humanity and nature as ends in themselves.

But in addition to these two forces in intellectual circles, there were important practical influences from the nonscholarly world of trade, commerce and politics which catalyzed the scientific revolution. To begin with, the sixteenth century saw a rapid growth of mining and metallurgy in southern Germany, which was linked by the Rhine to the advances in weaving technology then taking place in Flanders. It was along this same trade route that Gutenberg worked to perfect his printing press, and then to search for the right kinds of metal alloys for molds in which to cast its movable type. Additionally, sixteenth-century Portuguese and Spanish exploration presented new challenges to astronomy, mathematics and instrumentation in the course of reaching the New World, and to medicine, agri-

Tech. need ——> sc of that

(4)

culture and biology in dealing with what was discovered there.

Finally, the Protestant Reformation touched off a series of wars for which gentleman officers needed the mathematical knowledge associated with manning fortifications and using guns. These wars in turn bred new kinds of military practitioners, such as engineers and surgeons. All of this led to a state of affairs in which the "applied mathematical arts" (formerly seen as the province of commoners only) became a standard part of every Continental gentleman's education by the seventeenth century. The eighteenth-century Industrial Revolution in Europe led to the gradual replacement of independent, home-based craftsmanship by mechanized, centralized factories. This shift was aided at least indirectly by experimental methods borrowed from the developing natural sciences. In turn, the new problems generated by industrialization provided both incentives and consumers for scientific research.

We can thus see that the development of natural science in seventeenth- and eighteenth-century Europe was preceded and to a large extent justified by the development of technology, commerce and empire building in the sixteenth century—so much so that one historian remarks that natural science's "roots in thought and society are the same as those of European technology and of its acquisitive spirit; science is an important part of the process that achieved domination for this small, and, until recently, barbarous corner of the world."[3]

Natural science as the servant of secularism. We have already said that the resentment toward sixteenth-century ecclesiastical authority was one of the factors giving birth to the scientific revolution of the seventeenth century, and that the renaissance of Greek and Roman cultural expression was a second. Both these influences helped launch a spirit of secularism in Europe according to which the universe was regarded less as the creation of a personal, biblical God to whom humanity was morally accountable and more as merely matter, morally neutral and able, in theory, to be exhaustively described in purely mathematical terms. In the mideighteenth century the intellectual movement known as the Enlightenment continued this process of secularization, using the facts of science and its rational method as its chief weapons. In point of fact, the greatest prophets of the scientific revolution (such as René Descartes in France and Francis Bacon and Isaac Newton in England) saw in their scientific achievements new possibilities for the support of traditional religion. But the leaders of the Enlightenment in France, committed to a struggle against popular superstition, church dogma and a state censorship system of ridiculous proportions, saw in Newton's grand effort to unite the heavens and Earth in one impersonal law of gravity a splendid platform for their ridicule of the status quo in politics and religion. All agreed that natural science was, by its very nature, an essential ingredient in the ideology of the French Revolution and the subsequent establishment of the Republic. Far from being neutral and objective, science was perceived as a political and philosophical servant of antichurch, antiroyalist concerns.

The appeal to science as an aid in undermining traditional biblical cosmology continued in nineteenth-century Britain with the emergence of geology and its questioning of what was taken to be the biblical record of Earth's history. It was also furthered by Darwin's theory of evolution, which challenged the doctrines both of creation and of humanity's uniqueness before God in distinction from the animal kingdom. Darwin's theory was also adapted as an explanatory principle by the newly emerging social sciences, many of which began to use the evolutionistic metaphors of "environmental pressure" and "survival of the fittest" to account for changes in political, social and economic institutions.

In retrospectively assessing the antichurch struggles of Galileo in the seventeenth century, the followers of the Enlightenment in the eighteenth, and the Victorian-era intellectuals of the nineteenth, it is important that twentieth-century Christians not fall into the error of simplistically idealizing either side of the struggle. On the one hand, the emerging natural sciences had a legitimate complaint against the established church's attempts at interference in their development.[4] On the other hand, many people, both in the center and at the fringes of early science, eagerly used its metaphor of a totally mechanistic, impersonal universe and a humanity completely passive in the face of environmental pressure and genetic mutation to justify the casting off of _all_ traditional moral restraints and authority relationships. "If God does not exist," warned Dostoevsky in his _Brothers Karamazov_, "anything is permitted." Similarly, if human beings (as many of Darwin's popularizers insisted) are destined only to a meaningless, animal-like struggle for the survival of the fittest, then one need no longer exercise any moral self-restraint in either personal relationships or political activities. There might be things which for pragmatic reasons a person will refrain from openly supporting or doing—because he realizes that a reactionary society still harboring the illusion of moral accountability simply will not tolerate them. But in principle, "anything is permitted" that one can get away with. The twentieth-century writer Aldous Huxley, himself the descendant of a distinguished, pro-Darwinist family, was uncommonly honest in his later life about his own motives for embracing such a world view:

> I had motives for not wanting the world to have a meaning; consequently I assumed that it had none, and was able without any difficulty to find satisfying reasons for this assumption. The philosopher who finds no meaning in the world is not concerned exclusively with a problem in pure metaphysics; he is also concerned to prove that there is no valid reason why he personally should not do as he wants to do, or why his friends should not seize political power and govern in the way that they find most advantageous to themselves. ... For myself, the philosophy of meaninglessness was essentially an instrument of liberation, sexual and political.[5]

Others, while recognizing the potential for unchecked, dog-eat-dog competition as a result of a mechanistic, evolutionistic approach to history, nevertheless insisted that this competition need not be permanent. All that was needed, they said, was the right kind of scientific education at the hands of the right kind of enlightened, rational planners to produce a new breed of children whose characters would be so shaped as to render them virtually incapable of harming others in the course of pursuing their own interests.

Bertrand Russell, the British mathematician and philosopher, was perhaps the most prolific and visible advocate of this faith in the unlimited possibilities for a happier, more truly moral humanity to be realized by a knowledge of natural science methods, rationally applied. In his 1930 essay, "The New Generation" (the preface to a multiauthored book of essays by the same name), he appeals to "scientific power," "growth of knowledge," "enlightened people," and "the care of experts" in almost every paragraph as means of rearing children of the new age. No longer was religious socialization necessary—indeed, religion (by which he meant Victorian-era Christianity) in the past had only served to perpetuate unscientific superstition and to repress the natural curiosity of children. By contrast, rationally applied science could produce people from whom moral behavior would flow automatically. "It has become clear," he wrote, "that while the individual may have difficulty in deliberately altering his character, the scientific psychologist, if allowed a free run with children, can manipulate human nature as freely as Californians manipulate the desert. It is no longer Satan who makes sin, but bad glands and unwise conditioning."[6] It should come as no surprise that one of the contributors to this volume of essays was pioneer American psychologist J. B. Watson, whose legacy in behaviorism remains a dominant force in psychology to this day.

The Emergence of Psychology as a Separate Discipline

The word *psychology*, from the Greek *psyche* ("soul") and *logos* ("word," "speech," or "account"), comes closest to its original meaning when defined as the study, knowledge or science of the soul. Philip Melanchthon, a collaborator of Martin Luther, is credited with coining the term in the midsixteenth century, but in fact philosophers have endeavored to understand and explain human nature and mental life since at least the classical Greek era beginning five centuries before Christ. The psychologically oriented part of philosophy has historically included all the ideas and solutions offered by philosophers to explain human nature, mind, consciousness and mental processes such as sensation, perception, learning, thinking, willing and feeling.

All these mental processes continue to concern psychologists today, although the first half of the list receives somewhat more attention than the latter half. The following pages will offer a brief outline of the history of psychology, both before and after its separation from its parent discipline of philosophy, followed by a description of some of the changes that took place in the wake of that separation and psychology's decision to pattern itself after the natural sciences. We will conclude this opening chapter by listening to some voices raised in unsuccessful protest against this decision, and then by suggesting *why* the decision to model the discipline after the natural sciences was so readily adopted by psychology.

Metaphysical and prescientific psychology. Histories of psychology often divide the development of the discipline into three fairly distinct eras.[7] The first of these, spanning more than two thousand years from classical Greece until the end of the Middle Ages, is called the *period of metaphysical psychology*. During this time, philosophers and church scholars of a psychological bent were, as the roots of the word *psychology* suggest, mainly concerned with theorizing about the nature of the soul and its relationship to the body. Most often the word *soul* was used with reference to religious and moral sensibilities, although sometimes it included other mental processes such as sensation, cognition and emotion. But in any case, methods of investigation were *deductive*, in that descriptive and explanatory schemes were developed and elaborated on the basis of prior religious or philosophical assumptions. The methodology of this era was also nonempirical in that such schemes were not usually based on the observed experience of actual people but rather on the scholar's own rational reflections about the issue.

The second period, from about 1600 until the midnineteenth century, saw a shift in both content and methodology. In terms of content, psychology, although still a subgroup of philosophy and not yet called by its own name, became preoccupied chiefly with mental processes such as sensation, perception and the process of associating ideas, to the exclusion of matters pertaining to the soul. In dealing with these topics, it began to be influenced more and more by the methods of the developing natural sciences such as physics, biology and later physiology. This led to psychology's becoming more *empirical* in the most general sense of the term: that is, it began to build up its body of knowledge by studying actual experiences of persons observed firsthand. In other words, philosophers of a psychological bent began to look outward to the rest of the world in their study of mental processes, rather than inward to their own musings, in order to support their conclusions. In terms of methodology, psychology also became more *inductive*, in that from the data of observed experience it tried to find some general pattern. That is, rather than working from a presupposed pattern or structure accepted on the basis of past authority and fitting observations to this pattern, scholars now tended to reverse these steps: first they observed particular details and then reasoned from these to a more general pattern or structure. Because the use of an empirical, inductive methodology was so characteristic of the natural sciences, and because psychology was gradually adopting these methods in preference to the rational, deductive methods of philosophy, this era might be termed the *period of prescientific psychology*.

Psychology was moving toward, but had not yet fully espoused, a natural-science methodology.

The era of scientific psychology. The third and still current era, beginning with the opening of the first psychology laboratory in 1879 by Wilhelm Wundt in Leipzig, may be called the *period of scientific psychology*. During this era a number of trends which had begun to develop in the previous, prescientific era took more formal shape and eventually resulted in psychology's becoming an academic discipline distinct from philosophy. Early in the period, emergent psychology began to have more and more contact with physiology, that nineteenth-century off-spring of biology which studies the activities and functions of living matter and its associated physical and chemical reactions. Historians of psychology routinely agree that the influence of physiology was the single most important factor leading to psychology's separation from philosophy and its determination to be accepted as one of the natural sciences.

There are at least two reasons for this attraction of psychology to physiology. First, it began to be seen in the latter half of the nineteenth century that, due to the often complementary nature of psychological and physiological functions, mental processes needed to be studied at least partly with reference to the brain, nerves and sense organs. Philosophy alone could not achieve a complete understanding of the human mind. For instance, the long-held philosophical theory that an immaterial energy called "animal spirits" was responsible for muscle movement received a lethal blow when physiologists discovered the electrochemical nature of the nerve impulse. Second, late nineteenth-century pioneers of the newly established science of psychology were often physiologists before they began to call themselves psychologists. This was the case with both the acknowledged founders of the new discipline, Wilhelm Wundt in Germany and William James in America. Indeed, the new field of study was initially called "physiological psychology," not in the current sense of the term designating one aspect of psychology, but to describe what was assumed by its early practitioners to be its entire mandate.

Expanding the demands of empiricism. A second prescientific trend in psychology which became more deeply entrenched in this third, scientific period was the use of empiricism as a methodology for studying mental processes. But whereas the more general empiricism of the second era merely stressed an outward-looking appeal to observed experience (as opposed to armchair theorizing), empiricism now grew rapidly to include all the methodological trappings of nineteenth-century natural science. What, then, were some of these trappings?

They included, first of all, a stress on *reductionism*, the assumption that complex states and processes should be broken up into the smallest possible components. This was based on the further assumption that a right understanding of the whole could only be gained by studying the parts first in isolation from, and then in relation to, one another. Hence, because sensations such as hearing, seeing, tasting, touching and smelling were at that time held to be the smallest basic units of mental functioning, it is not surprising that the newly established psychology devoted disproportionate and painstaking attention to such topics.

The expanded definition of empiricism also included a demand for *experimentation* as the most promising route to psychological knowledge. That is, psychological functions were to be manipulated under controlled, carefully specified conditions in order to determine their causal antecedents. A much-heralded exemplar of this approach was Pavlov's experimentation with conditioned reflexes. In his experiments, performed in Russia at the turn of the century, he showed first how the introduction of meat powder into a dog's mouth led to salivation, and later how the pairing of the meat powder with the sound of a bell eventually led to salivation following the bell sound alone.

The experimental method was intended to lead to the *explanation* of psychological events. By determining how these events could be reliably produced, psychologists hoped to gain predictability and control over them. Mere description of psychological processes was more and more considered prescientific, inasmuch as it did not show how such processes could be predicted, produced and manipulated. To return to the example of Pavlovian conditioning, merely describing in detail the naturally occurring process of salivation in a dog outside the laboratory would, by these expanded criteria of empiricism, be regarded as second-class science, whereas the discovery under controlled conditions of factors which produce (and hence lead to the predictability and control of) salivation was celebrated as a true scientific advance.

Furthermore, in order to conduct valid experiments verifiable by others, *operationalization* of both the manipulations and the results of experiments was needed. Operationalization calls for specifying, preferably in quantitative form, experimental manipulations and their resulting observations in what might be called cookbook terms—that is, in a way which can be repeated by any persons reading the experimental report as long as they have access to the needed materials and instruments. Thus Pavlov's manipulations included first the unconditioned stimulus (so many grams of a certain kind of meat powder) and later the conditioned stimulus (a gong of so many decibels loudness, such and such a number of cycles per second pitch and so many seconds duration). His results were specified in terms of the number of milliliters of saliva produced in response to the presentation of meat powder alone, bell alone or both together. Notice that both the experimental manipulations and the subsequent results were operationalized—that is, specified in terms of precise materials used and actions undertaken by the experimenter—in order to allow for exact replication of the experiment by others.

Notice also that Pavlov's experimental manipulations and subsequent results were expressed in numerical terms. While it is possible for operationalizations to be purely qualitative (we will see an example of this in the next chapter), it has long been considered more scientific to express both manipulations and results in quantitative form. Moreover, this concern for quantification goes beyond the description of the individual subject's treatment and response to the corporate analysis of the behavior of all persons in the experiment. With the advent of that branch of mathematics known as statistics, it became more and more common to present in a summarized, numerical form the results of an experiment which had been performed on not just one, but a large number of animals or human beings. For example, the report of a series of experiments examining the conditionable nature of the human eyeblink might refer to the mean (or average) number of milliseconds delay before onset of the eyeblink. In such a statistical summary, individual performance is not only reduced to a number but disappears into a mean performance calculated by averaging the quantified performances of all participants in the study. With such a procedure the resultant average may in fact not describe the performance of any one of the individual participants in the study, any more than the statistic which proclaims that "the mean number of live children per American family is 2.2" describes any given American family! Nevertheless, the use of statistical procedures was to become even more common in psychology than in most of the natural sciences, simply because human behavior is subject to so much more fluctuation within and across individuals than is the performance of metals, chemicals or even isolated living tissues and organs. Hence it was held that the only way to express the essential results of any study was to summarize the performance of all the participants in a way which canceled individual differences.

A final feature of the expanded definition of empiricism was the criterion of objectivity as practiced by the natural sciences. This criterion demanded at least two things. First of all, it meant at the very least that human behavior and mental processes were to be studied in the same way the Newtonian physicist studies

force and matter or the biologist studies plants and animals—
not as one personal being making contact with another equally
personal being, but as a detached observer looking at something
essentially different from himself, something which has to be
figured out, like a puzzle, with only the data of the senses (seeing, hearing, touching, tasting, smelling) to provide hints. Sense
data was all that was available to the natural scientists from the
materials and living things which were their subject matter.
Consequently psychologists also argued the necessity for a rigid-
ly objective (in the sense of "detached" and "depending on the
senses") methodology in their research. In its assumption that
it had to mimic the approach and methods of the natural sciences, emergent psychology also took over these canons of objectivity, even though the main subject matter of psychology
is not something different from the investigator but rather an
entity like himself—a person whose range of behavior, thinking, feeling and valuing is not terribly different from his own.
The investigator could conceivably, if so inclined, compare his
subject's experience with his own in order to get further hints
as to its nature and functioning.

It is significant that to this day not only animal but also human
participants in psychology experiments are referred to as "subjects"—not in the sense of having valuable "subjective" personal input to contribute to the experiment, but in the sense of
being passively "subject to" the experimenter's manipulations.
This practice also reflects the methodological insistence on a
natural-science criterion of objectivity which requires that investigating psychologists treat the persons they study as essentially different from themselves, and perhaps even as less human or more objectlike than themselves. The fact that these investigators are probably quite personal and egalitarian in their
treatment of persons outside the laboratory does not alter the
fact that an entire science of persons is being constructed on the
basis of a methodology developed for work with nonhuman entities.

But the term *objectivity* came to connote another aim as well. Psychologists thought it both desirable and possible to observe what was "really there," quite independent of what might be personal or private in the investigator's feelings. This sense of the term *objectivity* called for an investigation and use of facts without distortion by personal feelings or prejudice. But such a requirement obviously leads to two other questions: What is to be regarded as a pure fact, and what is to be dismissed as mere prejudice, bias or private feeling? The expanded definition of empiricism was adamant about the answers to both these questions. "Facts" were based on what was available to the senses from the world "out there," whereas conclusions reached on the basis of anything else (such as imagination, faith, revelation or an intensely moving experience) were to be classed as subjective feelings which were at best useless for arriving at general laws because they were unique to their possessor, and at worst evidence of a self-centered arrogance which assumed that the meaning of the universe was somehow more able to be penetrated by one person than by others.

In the historical beginnings of the natural sciences, objectivity in this sense was invoked in opposition to the scholastic tendency to ignore the merely sense-observable features of the world in favor of concentrating on what was held to be their deeper, invisible spiritual significance. In all fairness, it is likely that the reactionary emphasis by some natural scientists on this type of objectivity was simply an attempt to balance the picture, since whatever ultimate religious significance the world has, it is at least capable of being investigated on the sense level as well. Indeed many Christian scholars, especially in the wake of the Reformation, were among the pioneers of natural science: they had come to believe, upon examining Scripture more closely for themselves, that the world, as God's creation, was essentially good and worthy of close attention. It was not something to be disdained or ignored as being in a less spiritual class than the products of contemplation or revelation, as the scholastics tended to think. Moreover, in contrast to the residual traces of Greek thought which held nature at arm's length as a godlike entity to be feared and worshiped, Christian scholars rightly came to regard nature as something given by God for human use and management. Hence their Christian convictions stimulated their participation in the development of modern science.[8]

But such a biblically based motivation was not the only one behind the development of natural science with its growing insistence on sense objectivity. Indeed, however prominent such Christian motivation may have been in early scientists such as Descartes, Bacon, Newton and Boyle, it was paralleled and quickly eclipsed by a very different motivation—namely, the spirit of secularism to which we have previously referred in our outline of the history of natural science. The eighteenth-century leaders of the Enlightenment were quite frank that their aim was to liberate human personality from any previous ties to supernatural powers or, for that matter, to authority of any sort. Their goal was an autonomous humanity intent on controlling its own destiny, and natural science, which had already accomplished so much since its beginnings, would guarantee such autonomy and control.

Was there any "objective" evidence that this could happen? How could there be, since it was an aim directed toward a yet-to-be-realized future, not merely a statement about sense-observable facts in the present? Yet it was a faith which was to become every bit as strong and intolerant as the Christian world view it dismissed as unscientific and authoritarian. The irony is obvious: to insist that Christian faith language about the world and its inhabitants be replaced by "objective" sensory data is, in fact, not to eliminate faith but to replace it with an alternative, competing faith—in human capacity to harness the universe and human destiny within it, and in the methods of natural science as the means of realizing these goals.[9]

In summary, the new era of scientific psychology aimed at a methodology which was empirical, not merely in the wider sense of "attending to experience," but also according to the natural-scientific canons of reductionism, experimentation, explanation, operationalization, quantification and objectivity. When taken as immutable, these six criteria characterize the school of *positivism*, which in one form or another dominated European philosophy of science from the midnineteenth century through the early decades of the twentieth, and which has been a dominating force in North American psychology up to the present. Positivistic philosophy holds that only sense-observable data can be accepted as fact, that the appropriate language of all scientific inquiry is that of mathematics and formal logic, and that the conduct of real science need not and must not include any kind of faith language concerning God or anything else. For the sake of conciseness we will use the term *positivism* to refer to that view of psychology which adheres to all of the six criteria.

Such a positivistic orientation to psychology reached its extreme form in the still influential school of *behaviorism*, which declared in the early twentieth century that it was both possible and desirable to develop a psychology of human beings making no reference at all to what went on inside their heads but focusing only on their externally observable behavior. The most extreme behaviorists limited the definition of behavior to the movement of muscles and the functioning of bodily organs as measured by scientific instruments. When operationalized like this, they maintained, behavior could be reliably observed and measured, whereas one could only theorize and argue after the manner of philosophers about the nature of such intangible, private experiences as love, hope, hostility, purpose, religious sentiments or the many other processes which the ordinary person might expect psychologists to study. At the time, few people questioned either the exalted view of the researcher's capacity to be consistently positivistic in studying fellow human beings, or the reduced and circumscribed picture of human beings demanded by such a practice.

Such an orientation, still remarkably strong in psychology, begs a host of questions: Are sense-observable entities the only psychological realities, even in the lives of scientists committed to working as if they were? Can we do justice to human psychological processes only in the language of mathematics and formal logic? Is a faith orientation of some sort merely an optional personal possession which can and should be left outside the classroom or laboratory like a coat hung on a hook, or is it an inescapable part of all humans which necessarily shows through, directly or indirectly, even in the products of their scholarship? These are questions to which we shall return later, but at this point we also wish to consider the very real existence of a consistent, antipositivistic minority trend in psychology from the time of its emergence as a separate discipline.

Dissenting Voices

Early in this chapter we referred to the fact that, from the beginning of psychology's identity as a discipline separate from philosophy, a minority of scholars have doubted the adequacy of a purely natural-science approach to the study of human beings. At this point we will look at some of these early protesters in more detail.[10]

Let us return to psychology's official birthplace and birth date, Germany in the late nineteenth century. The first academic to call himself a psychologist was Wilhelm Wundt, who opened a laboratory in Leipzig in 1879. He specialized in collecting reports of people's perceived sensations in reaction to an experimentally presented physical stimulus, such as a rotating disc of colors or a pair of weights held one in each hand. Wundt's almost exclusive preoccupation with psychological sensations experienced in reaction to physical stimuli reflected the reductionistic aspect of natural-science positivism, which held that sensations constituted the smallest, irreducible building blocks of mental life. To understand higher mental functions, it was held, one must begin with an exhaustive study of these minute sensations and build up a systematic "psychological edifice" from there.

Overlapping Wundt's lifespan (1832-1920) was that of another erudite and very productive German scholar, Wilhelm Dilthey (1833-1911), by training a philosopher and historian. Dilthey's prolific writings included a consideration of this new discipline of psychology which his homeland had spawned. Dilthey was very different from the new psychologists both in his approach toward the person and in the methods by which he thought that psychology should proceed in its study of human beings. As we have seen, the natural-science training of most early psychologists led them to approach persons as basically similar to the rocks, chemicals, plants and animals studied by natural scientists—that is, as speechless, passive recipients of both naturally occurring environmental events and planned laboratory manipulations. Dilthey, on the other hand, maintained that such an approach could not do justice to what was uniquely human, particularly to the human capacity for creativity, purposeful striving, choice and the formation of values. These human qualities imply that persons are not silent, passive respondents like chemicals before the actions of the laboratory worker or animals before a trainer, but rather active initiators of both thought and behavior, having at least a degree of freedom they can exercise over and above biological and environmental constraints. To do justice to this more complete view of persons, Dilthey said, the approach and methods of the natural sciences (Naturwissenschaften), developed to deal with the nonhuman world, are simply inadequate. The human sciences (Geisteswissenschaften) needed an approach and methodology which would be rigorous and systematic but not imitative of the natural sciences.

What were some of the features of this proposed human-science orientation? Instead of looking at mental life in reductionistic terms as the sum total of thousands of individual sensations or acts, the human-science approach would be holistic, seeing the basic unit of mental life as the total reaction of the thinking, feeling, striving self to a situation confronting it. Instead of stressing controlled experimentation with carefully isolated factors at a single point in time, the human sciences would recognize that all human phenomena are contextual—that is, embedded in an ongoing spatial and temporal milieu which gives them meaning and hence must be taken into account. Instead of striving for cause-and-effect explanations of mental processes in order to be able to predict and control them, human-science methodology would focus on understanding the nature of these phenomena on their own terms and for their own sake, without regard to what causes them or how they can be used to cause something else.

Instead of operationalizing situational factors and human reactions to them in precise but very limiting terms, human-science methods would have to tolerate ambiguity; that is, they would have to live with the realization that the essence of any situation or the human response to it cannot adequately be captured in cookbook terms allowing for facile replication elsewhere. Instead of minimizing individual differences and grouping individual performances together by dealing with data quantitatively, human scientists would analyze data in more qualitative, or descriptive, terms. Finally, in contrast to the objectivity required of natural scientists toward their nonhuman subject matter, a human-scientific approach would require empathy between the investigator and the persons being studied, an attitude suggesting both communication between similar entities (rather than detached study and control of a lower by a higher entity) and a need to penetrate beneath mere sense impressions —that is, to go beyond what is seen and heard on the surface of the interaction between the human scientist and the person being studied.

It is generally conceded that Dilthey clarified, as had no one else before his time, the distinctive character that might be possible for the human sciences.[11] Yet in pointing out the limitations of the natural-scientific approach to psychology, he was not suggesting that psychology join the humanities. Rather, he maintained, the position of the human sciences is somewhere between the natural sciences and the humanities. His philosophical work on the distinction between the natural and the human sciences was elaborated and continued by his followers, most notably his successor to the chair of philosophy at Berlin, Eduard Spranger (1882-1963); it continues to this day to be a strong influence in German psychological circles. In chapter three we will look again at its basic orientation—that is, at its holistic, contextual, understanding, qualitative, empathetic approach which was prepared to tolerate ambiguity.

Dilthey and Spranger, of course, were philosophers, not empirical psychologists, even by the broad definition of empiricism. But a German contemporary of Spranger, Max Wertheimer (1880-1943), was both an experimental psychologist and an opponent of reductionism. Unlike Wundt and his followers, who "atomized" consciousness into what they considered its smallest elements—sensations—and studied these exhaustively, Wertheimer emphasized that consciousness is normally of some whole configuration and almost never of its separate sensory elements. He first demonstrated this principle by way of a toy stroboscope, a primitive precursor to the modern motion picture, in which a series of still photographs shown in rapid succession created the illusion of movement. Human perceptions of either a stroboscope or a motion picture are never of a series of discrete images, analogous to Wundt's sensations—even if one knows that these are its basic constituents—but rather of a continuously moving whole. Hence the psychology which Wertheimer developed was called *Gestaltpsychologie*, or the psychology of "forms" or "whole configurations."

Subsequent Gestalt research showed that even animals perceive patterns and configurations rather than isolated elements. A rat or monkey who has learned to find food behind a two-inch circle rather than a one-inch circle will, if transferred to another pair of circles now two inches and three inches across, choose not the two-inch circle of the first situation but the relatively larger three-inch circle that he has never before seen. This showed, said the Gestaltists, that the animal had "endowed the pair of circles with a form quality which is transferred from one pair to another."[12]

In the same spirit Gestalt psychology also attacked early behaviorism which, inspired by Pavlov's experiments in conditioning, argued that all human learning is simply a chain of small habits, each serving as a stimulus to set off the next. By contrast the Gestaltists argued (and demonstrated) that sometimes learning appeared all at once, in the form of insight, rather than being built up piece by piece. One of Wertheimer's collaborators, Wolfgang Kohler, specialized in experiments with chimpanzees who, given a series of unfamiliar tools such as sticks and boxes, were able with considerable swiftness to obtain otherwise inaccessible food. Learning, like visual perception, need not be studied in isolated parts; greater understanding might come from examining the act as a whole.

These two examples show that the Gestaltists adopted some but not all of the positivistic criteria common to the natural sciences. They were empirical in their observation of the outside world and its inhabitants and experimental in their exploration and establishment of Gestalt "laws." They also operationalized their manipulations and observations in a way which could be repeated by others. But they were violently antireductionistic, were mostly content to describe rather than to explain and control phenomena, and usually presented their findings in qualitative rather than quantitative form. Their opposition to reductionism was directed particularly toward Wundt's approach, which Wertheimer dismissed as "brick-and-mortar psychology," meaning that it regarded experience as little more than a collection of sensory bricks held together by the mortar of association.

But in reality, Wundt himself was not the thoroughgoing natural-scientific psychologist he is usually made out to be. One of his reasons for concentrating his experimental work exclusively on sensations was that he did not find the experimental method adequate for the study of anything more complex. Indeed, in his later years he produced a ten-volume *Volkerpsychologie* ("Ethnopsychology") in which he consistently maintained that higher human thought processes could be understood only through a variation of the historian's methodology as applied to the study of language, art, mythology, religion, customs and law. Hence Wundt, normally hailed as the founder of natural-scientific psychology, also stands in the lesser-known tradition of psychology as a human science.

The same can be said of William James, routinely cited as a forerunner of behaviorism and the initiator of natural-scientific psychology in America. Although a physiologist by training and a strong advocate of positivism in his famous *Principles of Psychology* (one of the first psychology texts to be written and published in America), his later writings showed his concern for a holistic approach to human mental function in opposition to Wundt's reductionistic preoccupation with sensations. They also treated such human functions as will, reasoning and conscience, which were routinely dismissed by later psychologists because their study by positivistic methods seemed impossible. "James," writes one historian, "never lost sight of the total man. He tried to comprehend man's mental life as it is actually experienced." He was an empiricist in the broad rather than the narrow sense and "utilized any method that would shed light on man. With this approach, perhaps he was able to learn more about man than his narrowly experimental colleagues."[13]

In James's psychology, there was room for the unconscious, for the abnormal, and even for psychical phenomena and religious experience. Indeed, near the end of his life he produced a work entitled *The Varieties of Religious Experience* (1902) which, while not always well received by his experimentally inclined colleagues in psychology, was highly regarded by other academics and the educated reading public. It is noteworthy that during James's thirty-two-year tenure at Harvard, for only eight years in the middle of his career did he change his title from professor of philosophy to professor of psychology. Although he remained active in psychological circles until his death (he was one of only two people to have had two terms as president of the American Psychological Association), he apparently found the growing trend toward an exclusively positivistic approach in psychology too confining for his wide-ranging study of human experience. He spent his retirement years writing three famous philosophical volumes including *The Meaning of Truth* (1909).

Why Did Psychology Become a Natural Science?

The foregoing is far from an exhaustive account of the human-science tradition in early psychology. It is given merely to alert the reader to the existence of such a trend right from the discipline's beginning in Europe. Why then, in the face of such anti-positivistic influences, did North American psychology finally attach itself almost exclusively to a natural-science positivism with its stress on experimentation, explanation, objectivity, operationalization, reductionism and quantification?

Earlier in the chapter when we discussed the rise of natural science in seventeenth- to nineteenth-century Europe, we commented that both the rise of secularism and the rise of technology were influential factors. It is not an oversimplification to suggest that the same two factors re-emerged in nineteenth-century America as the primary determiners of the shape of twentieth-century psychology. To understand the impact of secularism—that is, the progressive decline of Christian belief—we need to remind ourselves of certain important features of life in seventeenth- and eighteenth-century colonial America.

Secularization and the rise of psychology.   In the first place, the majority of early settlers in America came here because they disagreed with the religious direction of their native lands, whether that direction were toward the establishment of a state church which was intolerant of nonconformist groups or toward a growing secularism. The colonists were consequently a serious-minded, religious people in whose limited intellectual life theology occupied a prominent position. In fact, before the rise of natural-scientific psychology in Germany, any psychology taught in American colleges and universities was called "mental philosophy" and was taught mainly by theologians. Psychology was of interest inasmuch as it shed light on the processes of conversion, sanctification, apostasy and spiritual struggle. Indeed, histories of psychology often cite Jonathan Edwards, the famous eighteenth-century preacher and author, as a precursor to modern psychology in his concern with psychological problems related to religion and his occasional use of what we would now call psychotherapeutic techniques on disturbed members of his congregation. As a result of such intense religious preoccupations, American philosophy (and with it, psychology) pursued a rather narrow range of topics until the midnineteenth century. It has been described as "a kind of Protestant scholasticism which derived its psychology from theological dogma."[14]

In the second place, before the Industrial Revolution's contributions to communication and transportation, America was largely cut off from intellectual developments in Europe, including the course of the scientific revolution and the trend toward secularism. Young men of an intellectual bent often had no socially approved way of developing their talents except by way of training for the ministry (and women, of course, had not even this). Consequently, of those who entered the ministry primarily for intellectual training rather than out of strong religious conviction, some not only left the church as soon as a viable professional substitute arose, but took with them a reactionary bitterness toward the religious training they had endured without wholehearted belief. For two of America's three pioneers in psychology (James being the exception), natural-scientific psychology appears to have provided both the substitute profession and the intellectual vehicle for rebellion against a religious upbringing.

G. Stanley Hall (1844-1924) earned America's first doctorate in the new psychology as taught by James at Harvard. Thereafter he was one of the most active contributors to the shape of American psychology as we know it today. He was the founder of the country's first experimental psychology laboratory, the founder and editor of the first psychology journal, and the organizer of the American Psychological Association in 1892, which, some ninety years later, boasts a membership of about 70,000 persons in forty different divisions of psychology. From a stern New England Puritan farm home, he went to Williams College and then to Union Theological Seminary, having been raised to see the ministry as the only vehicle for advanced study. However, Hall's undergraduate career began only four years after the publication of Darwin's *Origin of Species* (1859), and so captivated and convinced was he by the theory of evolution that he took it with him to seminary where, according to one historian of psychology, "after his trial sermon, the member of faculty whose custom it was to criticize, despairing of mere criticism, knelt down and prayed for his soul."[15]

Hall's devotion to evolutionism continued throughout his life, and his efforts to find in evolutionary principles a better understanding of human behavior earned for him the title (of which he was immensely proud) "the Darwin of the mind." He is described as being totally unable to tolerate the pre-Darwinian, theologically oriented psychology which had pervaded American philosophy prior to the midnineteenth century. He promoted the view that all childhood development could be understood as a recapitulation of the evolution of the human species; thus, for example, the climbing activities of toddlers were interpreted as a reversion to the prehuman, anthropoid phase of evolution. All historians of psychology credit Hall with tremendous gifts as a promoter, organizer and teacher; so it is hardly surprising that his commitment to evolution as a major explanatory principle of human thought and behavior is entrenched in North American psychology to this day, despite its overfacile generalization from biological development to the development of thinking, behavior and social organization. It is significant that even historians of psychology who normally show no propensity toward a religious interpretation of their subject concede that Hall's psychological evolutionism was more a faith commitment to a particular world view than a conclusion based on any kind of scientific research. "His devotion to evolutionary doctrine," writes one pair of historians, "approximated a devotion to religion, and the zeal with which he taught this doctrine was akin to the zeal of the most ardent religionists."[16]

Thus it is probably not an exaggeration to say that Hall helped launch natural-scientific psychology in America at least partly on the strength of his reaction to his strict Christian upbringing. To the extent that American Protestant scholasticism used the methods of philosophy to develop a psychology which would support church doctrine, Hall used the methods of natural science and a world view based on evolutionary theory to develop a psychology which would repudiate his past. In addition he supervised no fewer than eighty-one Ph.D. students in his lifetime. These constituted a substantial proportion of the vanguard of academic psychology all across America, passing on the positivistic, evolutionistic loyalties of their teacher.

There is some evidence that a similar personal history characterized the third first-generation pioneer of American psychology, G. T. Ladd (1842-1921), who graduated from Andover Theological Seminary and spent ten years in the ministry before becoming professor of "moral and mental philosophy" at Bowdoin College. However, he was attracted to Wundt's new physiological psychology when it emerged in the 1870s and began teaching it during a later appointment to Yale in 1881. His influence on American psychology was felt well into the twentieth century by way of his many clearly written, well-received textbooks, all of which reflect an evolutionistic and positivistic bent. To Ladd, the mind's function is to adapt the organism to its environment in the practical business of physical survival; of his evolutionistic convictions one writer comments that "the history of American psychology is little more than their working out in reality."[17]

There is evidence that, to this day, academic psychology in North America attracts persons who see in it a socially and intellectually acceptable way of evading, if not actually attacking, their Judeo-Christian heritage. A 1965 national survey of social scientists in university posts indicated that, even more than sociologists and political scientists, psychologists were indifferent or hostile to religion. Fully two-thirds of the psychologists interviewed said either that they were not at all religious or that religion was not a major force in their lives. But at the same time, when asked to indicate religious preference, only fifteen per cent said "none."[18] This apparent contradiction may well mean that most indicated the religious affiliation of their youth, to which they may still adhere for demographic or sociocultural purposes, but whose doctrines they have long since ceased to take seriously. On the anecdotal level, such an interpretation is supported by the reflections of one academic psychologist who became a Christian in midcareer:

> It is difficult to document such a thing as the general attitude of a profession. But the hostility of most psychologists to Christianity is very real. For years I was part of that sentiment; today it still surrounds me. . . . In graduate school, religion was treated as a pathetic anachronism. Occasionally a person's religious beliefs were "measured" in personality tests. The common interpretation was that people holding traditional religious views were fascist-authoritarian types.
>
> It is a curious hostility, for most psychologists are not aware of it. . . . The universities are so secularized that most academics can no longer articulate why they are opposed to Christianity. They merely assume that for all rational people the question of being a Christian was settled—negatively—at

some time in the past.[19]

In summary, I have tried to point out how the process of secularization in America—its arrival from Europe delayed by the inevitable culture lag—found in the natural-scientific psychology of the late nineteenth century an ideal means for its own propagation. By historical coincidence, the new psychology was imported to America just as first-generation apostates from orthodox Christianity were willing and eager to be its pioneers. In their efforts to sever the umbilical cord with a strongly religious upbringing, these founders of American psychology displayed the typical zeal of converts in assimilating and promoting their new faith in a positivistic, evolutionistic psychology, inaugurating a trend which continues to this day.

The impact of the technological mentality in North America. It was not, however, only the fortuitous meeting of the new secularism with the new psychology which determined psychology's identification with the natural sciences in North America. Early generations of colonists, for all their religiosity, were necessarily very practical people who had to spend most of their energies taming a frontier and forcing it to yield them a livelihood. Subsequent generations were of a similar practical nature as they continued to push the frontiers farther and farther west. This concern for practicality left an indelible stamp on the character of North American psychology. It is another major reason for its espousal of the natural-scientific method, with its potential for the explanation, prediction and control of phenomena in the natural world. What America wanted was a functional psychology, not one which stopped at mere description of the intricate structures of the mind. "We should be practical men and see to it that we have a practical psychology," urged J. N. Cattell, a second-generation American psychologist. From its earliest days, American psychology largely waved aside the question, "Of what does the mind consist?" (the so-called structuralist approach), and proceeded to the more pragmatic question, "What can the mind do?" (the so-called functionalist approach). Clearly evolutionism's stress on the survival of the fittest was in keeping with America's functionalist mentality in psychology, as was the promise of technological mastery offered by a natural-science methodology.

It is probably difficult for North Americans to appreciate how strange this practical, or functional, orientation in American psychology appeared in the eyes of European academics in the late nineteenth century. While it is true that the scientific revolution in Europe also served the interests of applied technology, by the nineteenth century natural science as an academic pursuit seemed to have matured into an enterprise much more concerned with knowledge of the world for its own sake than with any practical applications it might generate. Indeed, when Cattell, who went to Germany to study with Wundt, chose as his thesis topic the study of individual differences in reaction time (whose potential usefulness in education and industry impressed and excited him), Wundt showed no enthusiasm whatsoever and is said to have dismissed the topic as *ganz Amerikanisch* ("typically American"). Even more recently, a European psychologist of the stature of Jean Piaget marveled at America's preoccupation with the usefulness of his findings. While Piaget studied in intricate detail the quality of children's thinking at various stages of intellectual development, many of his American readers impatiently bypassed the details of each stage in order to ask him if there was any way to accelerate progress through these stages. Piaget always called this query "the American question."

There is much evidence that "American questions" regarding the practical usefulness of psychology have continuously influenced the direction of the discipline and have contributed to its positivistic insistence on quantification, experimentation, objectivity and the other features of a natural-science methodology. In 1921, a mere three decades after the official birth of psychology, Cattell (whom one historian calls "psychology's businessman") established the Psychological Corporation, whose stated aim was "the advancement of psychology and the promotion of the useful applications of psychology."[20] Among its twenty original directors were two of the three first-generation academic pioneers of American psychology, G. S. Hall and G. T. Ladd (James had by this time died).

But even before this, America's entry into World War 1 in 1917 supplied an opportunity for the fledgling discipline to justify its existence in terms of the sudden and urgent demands of the war effort. Academic psychologists were called in to research troop morale, military instructional techniques, mental breakdown created by battle stress, and visual and auditory perception as they related to the conduct of battle. But perhaps the most challenging and exciting assignment for scientific psychologists of a practical bent was to devise valid, efficient, objective tests by which almost two million men were to be classified and allocated to various military assignments. The resulting "Army Alpha" test (for literate persons) and its corresponding "Army Beta" (for illiterates) became prototypes for the postwar proliferation of intelligence, aptitude and personality tests in education and industry. Moreover, this mass testing of draftees gave psychologists their first chance to investigate behavior and mental functioning using large numbers of individuals who did not have to be consulted about whether they wanted to participate in such research. This opportunity—one of the fortunes of war—may have spoiled psychologists, leading them to expect in peacetime the same easy access to captive research populations in schools, colleges and other institutions, an access they have continued to exploit with very little questioning until recently.

From the 1920s to the present, American psychology has ridden high on the successes of its wartime contributions. Its development as an academic, natural-science-oriented discipline was intricately interwoven with its development as a profession—so much so that it has often been hard to detect any clear boundary between the two.[21] Public interest in the potential contribution of psychology to education, business and industry has remained high. Textbooks in applied psychology began to appear in the twenties, when many academic psychologists began to offer professional services as consultants. During World War 2, the volume of academic publications plummeted as the universities were almost emptied of psychologists, 1500 of whom were engaged in the war effort. Their assignments were generally similar to the ones they had pursued in the First World War, although they were conducted with the increased sophistication that one would expect from the intervening twenty years of psychology's development. This time psychologists were also called upon to develop and administer a personality assessment program for the selection of intelligence personnel who would be establishing and training resistance groups, disrupting enemy morale and procuring information behind enemy lines. One can argue, even from a Christian standpoint, for the cultivation of such routine duplicity in a wartime effort aimed at defending the sovereignty and freedom of nations. But it is also possible that, as in World War 1, psychologists simply assumed that their wartime powers would follow them back to their peacetime university posts. In the following chapter we will examine the presumption of many experimental psychologists that routine deception in the course of research is a necessary and justifiable practice.

But before we do this, let us briefly retrace the terrain covered in this chapter. We began with a brief look at the history of natural science from the sixteenth through the eighteenth centuries in Europe, pointing out how the forces of secularism and the development of technology aided its progress. We then considered the history of psychology in its metaphysical period up to the end of the Middle Ages, followed by its prescientific and scientific periods during which it ceased to examine human nature for purely religious reasons and instead began more and more to adopt the positivistic approach of the natural sciences with their stress on reductionism, experimentation, explanation, objectivity, operationalization and quantification. We saw that, particularly behind the scientific insistence on objectivity, there lay a new and largely unarticulated faith which had replaced the traditional Christian faith in a Creator to whom humanity was answerable: a faith in the human capacity to understand and control the world through the methods and findings of science. This was a faith which most psychologists only too eagerly adopted, with only a minority of dissenters questioning the application to human beings of a methodology developed for use with nonhuman aspects of nature. We concluded with a look at the history of natural-scientific psychology in North America, pointing out that the forces of secularism and technological pragmatism which had influenced the rise of science in Europe were "writ large" in the development of psychology in America. In particular, it appears that certain of the most influential pioneers in American psychology found in it an ideal vehicle for renouncing their own Christian upbringing in the name of science; in addition, the traditional American concern for practical aids to survival and for the development of the nation offered further reasons for the new psychology to develop along the lines of the natural sciences. In the following chapter, we will consider the outcome of this alliance which was undertaken with such initial confidence.

CHAPTER 2

THE APPRENTICESHIP UNFULFILLED

CHAPTER ONE DESCRIBED in some detail the way in which North American psychology came to attach itself to the natural sciences. Pursuing the analogy of the sorcerer's apprentice introduced at the beginning of chapter one, we may now ask whether psychology has been able to apply successfully the magical tools of its chosen master. If the answer to this question is yes, then we should expect to have from psychological research a coherent, steadily growing body of reliable and useful laws regarding human behavior and mental processes in much the same way that research in physics and chemistry seems to lead to a coherent, growing body of reliable and useful laws regarding subhuman phenomena. If, on the other hand, the answer is no, then we might expect to see in the conduct of psychological research some of the same confusion and helplessness that characterized Goethe's apprentice sorcerer when he found that he could not control the very magic which he had activated in the first place.

In order to establish which of these answers is the more accurate one, let us first backtrack for a moment and recapitulate the features of a thoroughly positivistic, natural-science approach in psychology. Having done this, we will then explore the consequences of this approach by describing and evaluating an example of its full-blown application to the study of some significant human activities. More specifically, we will try to establish first whether this positivistic approach was *successful* in terms of generating reliable psychological laws, and second whether it was *acceptable* in terms of the moral standards regarding human behavior to which Christians (and non-Christian humanists) usually adhere. In this way, we may begin to work toward some conclusion regarding the outcome of psychology's apprenticeship to the natural sciences.

In the previous chapter, I gave considerable attention to what I called "the expanded definition of empiricism." Whereas empiricism in its original sense merely meant "attending to experience," the use of this term in North American psychology today almost always assumes six very strict rules of thumb for doing research. These include the use of *experimentation, operationalization,* and *quantification;* they also include the belief that natural science should be characterized by *reductionism* and *objectivity* and should have as its goal the cause-and-effect *explanation* of natural (including psychological) events.

In the North American context of today, it is not unfair to say that only when psychological inquiry has adhered to these six criteria has it been accorded the status of first-class research, with all that this implies regarding funding, publication and academic recognition. Research which deliberately departs from any one of these norms is given much less attention, and deliberate departure from two or more is courting professional ostracism. I use the word *deliberate* because it is routinely acknowledged that certain questions in psychology cannot, for instance, be subjected to the test of controlled experimentation leading to a clear and reliable explanation. The subject of intelligence as measured by IQ tests is a case in point: we simply cannot breed human beings like plants or animals and raise them in controlled environments in such a way as to settle, once and for all, the enduring question as to whether prenatal genetic inheritance or postnatal training contributes more to adult intelligence. In such cases, it is deemed acceptable—if regrettable —to stick as closely as possible to the remaining standards for positivistic research.

But even this concession is usually made with the implicit understanding that where ethics forbid deliberate experimentation, the researcher should be ready to exploit the fortuitous occurrence of what are called *naturally occurring* experiments. Hence, while we cannot follow the deliberate route of producing babies with identical genes, then exposing them to different upbringings to see if their IQs will differ in adulthood, it occasionally happens that identical twins, orphaned or born out of wedlock, are adopted into different homes. Provided that both twins can be followed up equally easily by the researcher, such a fortuitous situation can be classed and used as a naturalistic experiment which, while still not amenable to all the controls of a planned laboratory experiment, is deemed to be the next best thing.

If these six criteria of positivistic natural science are strictly enforced in psychology, it would seem to follow that research adhering to them must yield an especially thorough and reliable understanding of human psychological processes. Certainly this success has seemed to follow when natural-scientific methods have been applied to the study of nonhuman aspects of the world. How, for instance, could we ever have harnessed nuclear energy without a host of painstaking laboratory experiments and calculations by many physicists? How could we ever have conquered smallpox or wheat rust without a strict adherence to these rules of natural-scientific research?

On one level, these are persuasive arguments for the use of positivistic, natural-science methods. We should therefore take a close look at what happens when these methods are faithfully applied to the study of human psychological processes. This we will do in the following pages, by way of a detailed look at a representative piece of research from the area of social psychology.

There are good reasons for choosing to examine the success of the natural-scientific approach by examining an experiment in social psychology. It is not just that this is the area of my own training in psychology and hence one with which I am particularly conversant. Social psychology is also an area for which many people have had high hopes. Not only did it originally aim to study human behavior in the broader social context (surely a laudable goal), but to do so in a way which was firmly scientific according to our six criteria and hence capable of generating reliable laws of human psychological functioning. Furthermore, it is an area of psychology which has tended to attract persons of a liberal, social activist bent who wish to do research on socially relevant issues, such as prejudice, conformity, altruism, cooperation, competition, attitude change, group dynamics and a host of other seemingly important phenomena.[1] Hence many have expressed confidence that in social psychology the twin goals of rigor and relevance can be combined. Consequently, it seems a logical area in which to test out the two questions posed in the second paragraph of this chapter—namely, how *successful* is the positivistic approach in generating reliable psychological laws, and how *acceptable* is it, morally speaking, for use with human beings?

A Representative Experiment: "Misery Loves Company"

I have chosen this study, one which is often cited in discussions and texts, as a good example of research on the social psychology of group affiliation—that is, the psychology of how persons tend to come together and stay together in groups. The originator of this study, a well-known social psychologist named Stanley Schacter, resolved to turn an old common sense proverb, "Misery loves company," into an experimentally testable hypothesis.[2] In other words, he wanted somehow to turn the experience of misery into a precise, operationalized form (that is, into a sort of recipe that could be repeatedly followed in experiment after experiment). He also wanted to see if persons exposed to this misery tended, as a result, to seek the company of other people in a way which could also be precisely operationalized, preferably in the form of some measurement. How then did he go about this?

In his basic experiment, after which many subsequent ones have been patterned, Schacter used undergraduate female psychology students who had come to his laboratory in order to fulfill one of their course requirements—namely, spending a given number of hours as research participants, or "subjects," in the ongoing work of psychology professors or their graduate students. Each of these students was randomly assigned to one or the other of two experimental groups. The first group of students was asked to assemble in a classroom where a stern-looking man in a white coat introduced them to an impressive piece of apparatus which, he explained to them, was an electric shock generator. He explained to them that the purpose of the study (which was not its actual purpose at all) was to explore the students' pain responses to progressively more intense shocks—a prospect calculated to make them feel very miserable indeed when they were told about it.

On the other hand, the second group of students was assembled before the same man and the same apparatus at a different time, but informed in a relaxed and reassuring manner that although the experiment did have to do with their responses to electric shocks, these shocks would be so mild as to produce only a slight tickle or tingle—not a very miserable prospect at all. It was announced to each group that there would be a ten-minute break before the shock phase of the experiment began, and that each student had the choice of spending this waiting period either alone in an available cubicle with an easy chair and a magazine, or in the company of the other participants in an adjoining classroom. Recall that the original, true purpose of the experiment was to find out if misery loves company. Hence the experimental question: Were the students who expected to be receiving severe shocks more inclined to choose to wait in the company of others slated for similar stress, rather than alone? And were the students who anticipated no real stress more inclined to wait for their mild shocks without the company of others? The answer to each of these questions, after a head count of the choices made by each group, turned out to be yes: thus (it was concluded) the original hypothesis that misery loves company was verified.

Before we detail the scientific structure of this experiment and evaluate it in terms of both its methodological success and its ethical acceptability, a few clarifying remarks are in order. It must be understood that the young women in the experiment never actually received the electric shocks, mild or severe, to which they were told they would be exposed. Once they made their choices to wait alone or in company, they were told that the experiment was over and what its true purpose was. The methodological purpose of the shock stories was twofold: first, they were presented to produce in each group of women a particular degree of misery (a high degree in one group, a low degree in the other) in anticipation of the shocks they believed they would receive; second, the students were told that the experiment was about a topic (reaction to shocks) which it was not about at all in order to insure that the experimental misery manipulation would really work. For if the students had been truthfully told that the real purpose of the experiment was to examine their company-seeking behavior after inducing in them a state of high or low misery, then they would (it is reasoned) be able to think about the experimental situation and possibly control their reactions to it. By contrast, being ignorant of the real purpose of the experiment—in fact, being told something totally different—they would not have a chance to arrange premeditated reactions, but would rather react as naively and spontaneously to their misery as they presumably would in a real-life situation.

It must also be understood that the conduct of this experiment is in no way unique; indeed, I chose it because it is quite typical. It is routinely the case that college students, particularly psychology students, participate in psychology experiments, sometimes with very little choice in the matter if participation is part of a course requirement. It is also routinely the case that the participants in experiments are given incomplete and sometimes actually misleading information about the nature of the experiment in order to insure that they react in a spontaneous, unpremeditated way to the experimental manipulations. Experimenters, of course, are expected to debrief the participants afterward—that is, to explain the true nature of the experiment to them once their spontaneous reactions have been elicited and recorded. Finally, it is also a common practice that the experimental manipulation induces at least temporary stress in the participants. In this case, the participants did not actually have to endure the physical stress of shock, but certainly at least the one group of women endured the psychological stress of believing that they would be painfully shocked. The experiment was explicitly designed that way, in order to see if misery loves company.

These are points to which we will return shortly. But first let us be clear about the ways in which this particular experiment tries to meet the six criteria of positivistic science. Let us take these six criteria one at a time, showing how each is embodied in Schacter's study and making some critical comments on the use of each.

First, Schacter's attempt to determine if misery loves company is clearly a deliberately contrived, carefully executed *experiment*. One might well ask, given the frequent occurrence of unplanned misery in the world, why Schacter did not choose merely to make detailed observations and have in-depth conversations with various people who happened to be suffering misery as the result, not of experimental manipulation, but rather of the spontaneous ups and downs of everyday existence. To this query, the usual reply is that such a strategy would not yield the predictability and control afforded by a planned experiment. To simply observe that misery and company seeking often seem to go together in everyday life would take us no further than the original proverb itself: the mere coincidence of two events does not necessarily mean that the one caused the other to happen. To establish a causal relationship, natural-science norms demand that we must set up a controlled, isolated situation in which the one event (misery) is introduced and the other event (company seeking) is seen to follow, promptly and reliably.

Furthermore, the experimental task of establishing a lawful relationship between misery and company seeking is not an easy one. Indeed, psychology students intent upon an academic or even a clinical career are normally required to have taken entire courses in experimental design at both the undergraduate and graduate levels. For instance, the fact that we are going to compare the company-seeking behavior of a low-misery group with a high-misery group calls for certain precautions. For what if the first group just happened to be composed mostly of insecure freshmen, and the second group just happened to be composed of socially self-confident seniors? In such a case, we might expect the first group to be naturally more inclined to be shy and unsociable toward other people in the experiment, and the second group to be naturally more gregarious and company seeking, regardless of any difference in misery manipulations from the experimenter. Hence, finding that the low-misery (freshman) group was less inclined to seek company than the high-misery (senior) group would be of no help in establishing the law that misery loves company, since it may not have been the degree of imposed misery but rather something else from outside the experimental situation which caused members of the first group to choose to wait alone and members of the second to choose to wait together.

To overcome such "confounds," as they are called, the researcher learns to assign the incoming participants randomly (e.g., by the flip of a coin) to one experimental group or the other before the experiment actually begins. This, of course (to pursue our example), would not change the number of shy freshmen or sociable seniors in the experiment as a whole—but it would probably insure that they are equally distributed, or mixed together, in each of the two groups, so that any overall difference in company-seeking behavior could truly be attributed to the misery manipulation and not to differences in the two groups which happened to be there before the experiment began.

This kind of precaution (random assignment of participants to groups) is especially necessary when doing psychological research with human beings. Animals, such as laboratory rats, for instance, can be inbred and raised in controlled settings to such an extent that any pre-experimental individual differences are minimized; human beings, on the other hand, bring unique histories to an experiment which can never be erased. They can only be mixed together by random assignment to conditions in such a way (it is assumed) that they will not contaminate or confound the results of the researcher's manipulations.

Because Schacter's study fulfills the criterion of controlled experimentation, with its random assignment of participants to groups, their exposure to two different misery manipulations, and the recording of their resulting company-seeking behavior, it also seems to meet the goal of *explanation*. For who could deny that, within this carefully controlled experimental situation, it must have been the different misery manipulations that led to different degrees of company seeking in each group? The behavior of each group has been explained (in the sense of showing what caused what) by the prior experimental conditions which were imposed on each. Are we consequently on our way to the establishment of a universal law of behavior which can be retrieved and used with the same certainty as the law of gravity or Archimedes' law? (For we have seen that this has been a major goal of North American psychology since it emerged as a separate discipline.) We will return to this question later, for it bears directly on the first major question of this chapter—how successful is the positivistic approach in realizing its stated aim of generating reliable laws of psychological functioning?

In the third place, Schacter's experiment was faithful to the positivistic norm of *operationalization*. Operationalization requires that research manipulations and observations be stated in terms that would allow anyone else to carry them out in exactly the same way. Hence, in this particular study, "degree of misery" was operationalized in a qualitative manner as "exposure to an announcement of impending electric shock." Indeed, the original journal article reporting the experiment would most certainly be required to include the actual scripts used by the man in the white coat as he spoke to each group of woman students. (One can still read extracts from these scripts in social psychology textbooks.) Likewise, "degree of company seeking" was operationalized in two ways: first, as "the number of students in each group who chose to wait with others," and second, as "the strength of each student's desire to wait with others." This individual "strength of desire to wait with others" was in turn operationalized in a way that could also be exactly repeated by anyone else doing the experiment: the students were asked to check off one alternative on a scale of statements ranging from "I wish very much to wait alone" to "I don't really care whether I wait alone or together," to "I wish very much to wait together."

This procedure also allows us to see how the experiment was faithful to the fourth criterion of positivistic research, that of *quantification*. Note that the individual responses of the students have disappeared first of all into a numerical head count of the number of students in each group who wanted to stay together. Second, even on the individual level, students were required to express their choices by choosing a single item on a one-to-five scale. This allowed the researcher to assign a number to each student's response (e.g., a "1" for very low desire to stay together, a "5" for very high desire, and a "3" for a "don't care" response.) The highly qualitative activity of company seeking is thus reduced to a set of numbers for statistical analysis.

In addition, something else should be noted about the process of quantifying experimental results: when it is said, in the final written account of the experiment, that "the high-misery group was more inclined to seek company than the low-misery group," this does not mean that, without exception, every single student who expected severe shock wanted to wait with others; nor does it mean that, without exception, every single student who expected only mild shocks preferred to stay alone. The experimenter has simply compared the percentages of students in each group who prefer to stay together. If it turns out, for instance, that eighty-five per cent of the high-misery students chose to wait in company, whereas only twenty per cent of the low-misery students made such a choice, it would likely be concluded (after appropriate statistical tests) that this is a significant difference which warrants the conclusion that the misery manipulations did indeed succeed. But (and this is a crucial distinction) this does not mean that they succeeded in producing in every participant the choice intended by the manipulation to which she was exposed—nor that in a repetition of the experiment they would be any more likely to do so. It merely means that in the high-misery condition a student would more likely (not inevitably) choose to wait with others, and in the low-misery condition a student would more likely (again, not inevitably) choose to wait alone.

What has happened here is that the individual participant's response has disappeared into a probabalistic generalization.

This is rather like the kind of generalization intended in the statement, "The average American family has two children," which clearly does not mean that every American family must have two children simply by virtue of being American, but only that if, for instance, you met an American couple abroad and guessed that they had two children at home, you would more likely (but certainly not inevitably) be correct than if you had guessed any other number. This is exactly what Schacter's experimental report meant (and nothing more) by the statement "The high misery group was more inclined to seek company than the low misery group." But it is very easy, given the historical record of the experimental method for producing results "without exception" when its subject matter is less than human, to conclude, when reading a report of an experiment using human participants, that here too *everyone* must have responded as expected to the experimental manipulations. This is a crucial point to which we will return later.

There remain two tests of the adequacy of Schacter's experiment according to our six criteria for positivistic research in psychology. These are the criteria of *objectivity* and *reductionism*. With regard to the first of these, it will be recalled that we earlier defined the term *objectivity* in terms of two attitudes. The first was "detachment," the attitude of looking at the experimental subject matter and participants from the viewpoint of an outsider trying to solve a puzzle rather than the viewpoint of a human being sharing a common, communicable experience with other human beings. The second of these attitudes was "lack of bias," the determination to see only what is really there, uncontaminated by subjective distortion. How are these goals for objectivity (detachment and lack of bias) stressed in Schacter's experiment?

In the first place, detachment is very much a calculated—indeed, a required—feature of the experimenter's actions and demeanor throughout the experiment. Following an exactly worded script, the experimenter gives instructions to the seated students, who listen, it is assumed, passively. There is no spontaneous give-and-take between experimenter and participants; although participants are asked if they have any questions before the experiment begins, these are answered, as much as possible, according to a predetermined script which never gives away the true purpose of the experiment or in any way reduces the level of anxiety which has been aroused in the students regarding the anticipated shocks. No small talk is allowed among the participants, as this might contaminate the purity of the misery manipulations.

An atmosphere is clearly established in which the participants are expected to listen to instructions in a docile, receptive fashion and to fill out the forms as directed. Any attempts on their part to initiate a discussion, prolong the question period or make extensive written comments on the response forms are quickly cut short by the experimenter. The experimenter may well be (indeed, probably is) a receptive and humane person who might happily enjoy a Coke with friends after the experiment. But within the context of the experiment, he wears a completely different hat: just as the chemist assumes a detached, impersonal attitude toward the passive chemicals he carefully manipulates in the test tube, so (it is said) must the experimental psychologist regard the members of species *homo sapiens* seated before him waiting to respond to the experimental conditions he imposes. That is the way of science, and the way of science (it is assumed) is the route to the understanding of human beings as surely as it is the route to unlocking the secrets of the non-human natural world.

How does the experimental procedure try to assure objectivity in its second sense of "lack of bias"? By deciding in advance on very precise, operationalized definitions of both misery and company seeking—definitions which could be understood and put into practice by any other researcher wishing to repeat the experiment—and faithfully adhering to these definitions throughout the experiment. For what if, instead, the experimenter had simply reported: "I made this group of students quite miserable and that group of students less so, and I discovered that the first group of students liked company better than the second." In such a case, the experimenter's own *ad hoc* attempts to create what he thought was misery and to measure what he thought might be an indication of company seeking have been used without explicit operationalization. How then can his operations be repeated by anyone else? No, it is concluded, we must have definitions of misery and company seeking which are easily understood, agreed upon and put into operation by all potential investigators of these topics. In that way the vague, subjective notions of any given researcher are kept at bay and there is common agreement as to what misery and company seeking really mean in the experiment.

Finally, in what way is the norm of *reductionism* adhered to in this experiment? At first glance this may seem difficult to assess. In chapter one we referred to reductionism as the belief that the only way to understand complex psychological processes is to start with an exhaustive study of their smallest building blocks—for example, sensations and reflexes—and to build from there. Yet in this study Schacter does not appear to be concerned with minute sensations and reflexes (indeed, he never even refers to them), but rather with the larger and more humanly meaningful processes of anxiety and affiliation. Yet he is indeed reductionistic, in a slightly different way: both human misery and human affiliation are topics which have engaged the minds of artists, composers, writers and theologians from the beginning of history. They are complex, multifaceted phenomena which, furthermore, take place in ongoing historical, material and social contexts, and not in isolated laboratories. Yet, in Schacter's experiment, misery becomes reduced to "the short-term anticipation of the physical discomfort produced by electric shocks," and company seeking to "a check mark on a one-to-five scale of an inclination to wait in a room for ten minutes with other participants in the experiment." Does not such reductionism do a gross injustice to the complexity of these two phenomena?

The answer to this question is certainly yes, and, when pressed, psychologists will admit that what one gains in precision and repeatability by operationalizing these phenomena, one loses in the drastic reduction—indeed, the trivialization—of their very human, historical and social complexity. "But," most will say, "look at the larger picture: in the natural sciences, the study of isolated enzymes in isolated bacteria eventually leads to a cure for a human disease; experiments with apparently trivial petroleum by-products eventually result in the creation of new fibers for clothing and textiles. So, too, psychologists —even social psychologists—must start by studying reduced, even apparently trivial, versions of the phenomena they wish to study, and eventually, through faithful adherence to the same research norms as practiced by natural scientists, they will build up a body of enormously significant and useful information about human psychological functions."

Is the Positivistic Approach Successful?

We have just said, in effect, that the entrenched allegiance to the positivistic approach in human psychological research is justified by its supposed explanatory potential. Just as controlled experimentation—with its attendant concern for objectivity, reductionism, operationalization and quantification—has resulted in increasing predictability and control over the nonhuman natural world, so, it is presumed, its careful, continuous use in the study of higher human activities will eventually result in predictability and control over even the most complex psychological processes. Quite apart from the question as to whether such total control of human behavior would be morally *acceptable* (a question to which we will return later), we want now to consider whether it is even *possible*.

The positivistic approach in science was evolved for use with entities very different from the thinking, choosing, active scientists who learned to apply it. The natural scientist sees the rock or tree—and even, for the most part, the animal—as being essentially a passive reactor to the physical and chemical events of the environment. Unlike the scientist who studies them, they cannot, as far as we can tell, think about or act upon their world; they can, it seems, merely react to it. This raises a crucial and oft-debated question: do human beings fall into this category of passive reactors to environmental (including experimental) events? If they do, then we would expect that we could adapt a natural-scientific approach to their study with very little difficulty. If they do not, then any attempt to apply that approach should begin to generate great problems. To see which is the case, let us return to our representative psychology experiment, Schacter's study on "misery loves company," and examine it on a somewhat deeper level.

The ghost in the machine.   To begin with, let us reflect on an aspect of Schacter's procedure which we earlier said was quite typical of psychology experiments with human beings—namely, his deceiving the students about the real nature of the experiment. Here we clearly have a feature added to the experimental procedure which is not practiced by scientists working with nonhuman entities. Who has ever heard of physicists lying to their iron filings, or physiologists to their frogs, about their experimental intentions? They do not have to lie; neither the iron filings nor the frogs can reflect on the manipulations they are undergoing in any way that will alter the intended effect.

But the realities of psychological research with human beings are different: experimental psychologists have always realized that if persons in an experiment know about the nature and purposes of the manipulations they are undergoing, they will often react differently than if they do not know about them. They are not, in other words, merely passive reactors to the researcher's manipulations, despite their imposed silence throughout the experiment and their apparent obedience to the experimenter's instructions. They are not, as one psychologist put it, merely somewhat "larger rats or slower computers," reacting totally mechanistically to conditions imposed by someone else.[3] If Schacter were to tell his female participants that his real interest was not reaction to electric shocks, but rather whether misery loves company, it is more than likely that they would all begin actively thinking about this topic. Some might say to themselves, "My goodness! If he's going to all this trouble to find out whether misery loves company, I'd better not disappoint him in my reactions!" Others might say to themselves: "So he thinks he can make us get together by frightening us with these electric shock stories—well, he's got a surprise coming!" Social psychologists have names for such spontaneous reactions on the part of experimental subjects: the first is sometimes called the *cooperative subject effect* and the second the *uncooperative subject effect*.[4]

Here we see our first, and most embarrassing, problem with the use of a full-blown, positivistic, experimental approach in human psychology. It appears that, for the participants in the experiment, knowledge is power. That is to say, once the participants know or even speculate about the true purpose of the experiment, they are no longer bound by the manipulations of the experimenter, but (unlike the rat or the computer) can exercise at least a degree of self-determination and countermanipulate their responses in accordance with their own desires. There is, in other words, a "ghost in the machine": by merely understanding the manipulative forces impinging upon them, human beings are at least partially able to transcend these forces in a variety of ways.[5] Philosophers, in referring to this process, speak of it as the *reflexivity* of the human agent.

The cat-and-mouse game. Given this serious limitation on the workability of the natural-scientific experimental approach with human beings—a limitation of which psychologists are only too aware—one might expect researchers to see limited usefulness in experimentation with human beings and, accordingly, to look for other methods by which to study them. In fact, in North American circles, most do not. So much is experimentation held to be the ultimate way by which to establish laws of human behavior that it is standard practice to try to get around the problem of the participants' knowledge of the experiment by simply lying to them about its real purpose. As we pointed out before, the assumption behind such routine deception is that, by distracting the participants' attention from the true manipulations of the experimenter, one can elicit from them a naive, uncalculated, automatic response to these manipulations. This is sometimes seem as a cat-and-mouse game between experimenters and their subjects: the latter are assumed to be constantly trying to figure out what is going on, while experimenters in turn try to come up with more and more plausible deceptions to keep them from finding out!

Can this added strategy of deception really succeed in turning human research subjects into passive, ratlike or robotlike respondents ("naive subjects," as they are called in psychology), thus preserving the usefulness of the experimental approach? Not indefinitely. For as more and more people discover, directly or by hearsay, that psychology experimenters usually lie, there will be fewer and fewer potentially naive subjects for such experiments. Rather, every participant will come to an experiment with his or her own private hypothesis about what is going on, disinclined to believe anything that the experimenter says by way of explanation beforehand. Thus the validity of any experimental results will be seriously jeopardized, since participants will be reacting to their own subjective perceptions of what the manipulations are rather than to the express manipulations prepared by the experimenter.

It is not as if the ultimately self-defeating nature of this practice has gone unnoticed in North American psychological circles. One prominent social psychologist, observing and participating in this kind of research over many years, finally wrote in one of the most prestigious psychology journals as follows:

How long . . . will it be possible for us to find naive subjects?

Among college students, it is already very difficult. They may not know the exact purpose of the particular experiment in which they are participating, but at least they know, typically, that it is *not* what the experimenter says it is. . . . The use of deception on the part of psychologists is so widely known in the college population that even if a psychologist is honest with the subject, more often than not he will be distrusted. . . . There are, of course, other sources of human subjects that have not been tapped, and we could turn to them in our quest for naiveté. But even there it is only a matter of time. As word about psychological experiments gets around in whatever network we happen to be using, sophistication is bound to increase. I wonder, therefore, whether there is any future in the use of deception.[6]

When these warnings were first voiced in the mid-1960s, the response of most researchers was merely to escalate the cat-and-mouse game: they spread their net wider in an effort to obtain experimental subjects who, unlike college students and middle-class people who read popular psychology, know nothing about the institutionalized nature of deception in the laboratory—working-class people, prison populations, children and Third World people, for instance. Quite apart from the *ethical* questions surrounding the use of deception and the recruitment of ever-more-naive research participants, there remains the *practical* question as to just how long this cat-and-mouse game between experimenters and their subjects can continue before the pool of nonsuspicious people is exhausted. Would it not be easier simply to admit that human beings are more than larger rats or smaller computers and therefore cannot very profitably be studied psychologically by a natural-scientific methodology which has been perfected for use on subhuman entities?

The exportability of experimental findings. There is another serious problem which plagues the experimental psychologist studying higher human processes. It will be recalled that, in our earlier description of the structure of Schacter's study, we spoke of the importance of assigning participants randomly to experimental groups in order to make their overall characteristics roughly equal before proceeding with the experimental manipulations. If this is done, it can then be safely concluded that any differences in the resulting behavior of the groups are truly due to the experimental manipulations and not to any differences which just happened to distinguish the groups at the outset. Hence, in Schacter's experiment, we can conclude that it really was the process of inducing greater misery in the one group that made them more likely to want to seek company than those in the other group.

What, now, can we do with this piece of information—with this little cause-and-effect "fact module" from a typical experiment in social psychology?[7] If, as we are repeatedly told, the goal of scientific psychology is the prediction and control of behavior, just how much can we use Schacter's results to predict and control people's tendency to seek company when they are miserable (assuming, for the moment, that we have satisfied ourselves that such a use of these results is morally defensible)?

The answer to this question appears to be, "Not very much." It is true that, within Schacter's particular experimental microcosm, a certain kind of misery tended to produce a certain company seeking. But let us take a second look at the structure of the experiment. First of all, its participants were all females. (Would males have behaved in the same manner?) Second, they were all undergraduate college students. (Would their non-college-educated peers have reacted in just the same way to the experimental manipulations?) Third, they were all from a particular university campus. (Would students from a neighboring college have reacted in the same way?) The reader can no doubt see my point. While the random assignment of participants to groups assures us that, within the confines of the experiment, misery loved company, we have to remember that the participants are hardly a representative cross section of all the people to whom we might want to generalize the experiment's findings. In other words, there is no built-in guarantee that the findings are exportable to a similar experimental effort using any other kind of participants. It is quite probable that some researchers somewhere (probably students earning a laboratory credit in a social psychology course) have repeated Schacter's experiment using other types of people and perhaps have found similar results. But generally there is neither the time nor the incentive to repeat such experiments using a great many different kinds of people in order to increase the exportability of their findings. Indeed, so usual is it for psychologists to discover the laws of behavior using almost exclusively students as subjects that it has become common to complain that we have a psychology of white male college sophomores, and nothing else. (Indeed, Schacter was somewhat unusual in his use of woman students.[8])

The exportability of findings such as Schacter's to types of people who differ from the original experimental sample is thus always an open question. But there are other kinds of limits to the generalizability of findings in psychology. Would Schacter's misery manipulations have worked, even with the subjects he did use, if the experiment had been conducted in the more ordinary setting of the college dorms instead of in the laboratory? This is the question of the exportability of results to other situations. We can also question their exportability to other times: would even the same groups coming to the same setting, but at another time of day or of the academic year, generate the same results as Schacter obtained at the time he did the study?

One might also question the exportability of Schacter's law to situations where misery and company seeking are not defined by the precise, yet reductionistic, operations used by him. There are, after all, a host of ways in which to be miserable, and an equally diverse number of ways in which to seek the company of others. Investigating all possible expressions of these two phenomena in an experimental fashion could turn into a lifetime research project.[9] In short, it appears that there are absolutely no guarantees regarding the transferability of experimental findings to any situation other than the one in which they were generated. Psychologists, of course, are not the only researchers to suffer from such uncertainties: biologists have long distinguished between the reactions of living things *in vivo* (in real life) and *in vitro* (in the test tube). Indeed, the differences between the two have forced biologists to look for help to the newer ecological sciences which deal with plants and animals in their natural settings.

Naturalistic experiments.   But, you may ask, could we not do the same in psychology? Could we not take our experiments out of the laboratory and into the real world, so that by performing them in less artificial settings we might increase the exportability of our findings to the real world? This too has been attempted. For example, psychologists have attempted to study altruism, or helping behavior, by actually staging mock (but realistic) fainting incidents in subways and other public places in order to see what kind of people, and under what circumstances, will come to the aid of the victim.[10] In some ways, this would seem to be the answer to many of our problems: not only are we increasing exportability of our findings by choosing a real-world setting for the experiment, but we also seem to be solving the problem of finding "naive" subjects; in such a "naturalistic experiment," as it is called, the participants do not even know they are in an experiment.

Yet methodologically, most of the problems regarding the exportability of such research findings still remain. Even if several mock faintings are staged, using different locations, different times of the day and week, and different types of "victims," the resulting findings regarding onlookers' helping behavior still cannot be reliably generalized beyond those kinds of neighborhoods, those times of the day or week, and those kinds of victims. Nor, of course, can the findings be generalized to types of altruism other than that represented by the act of going to the rescue of a fainting victim—which is clearly only one of hundreds of possible ways of expressing altruism. In addition, the cause-and-effect laws resulting from such field experiments are still limited to the probabilistic generalizations referred to earlier in this chapter. In other words, findings are expressed in statements such as: "The victim who carried a cane received spontaneous help on approximately ninety-five per cent of the staged fainting occasions"—a result which may make the reader feel relatively happier about traveling on the New York subway lines but which still does not guarantee that he or she will not be among the remaining five per cent who are ignored when seized by a fainting spell in a subway car!

Finally, even in the use of such naturalistic experiments the problem of increasing subject sophistication remains. As it has become more and more widely known that psychologists conduct such studies, more and more people, confronted with an out-of-the-ordinary event, have begun to suspect that they are unwitting and unwilling participants in a psychology experiment. Not only does this mean that in a real field experiment they will react according to their own hypotheses about the situation (thus contaminating the purity of the researcher's manipulations); it also means that more and more people will be inclined to ignore any unusual event—even a real emergency —and walk away from it on the assumption that "it's probably just a psychology experiment." One is reminded of Aesop's fable about the shepherd boy who, bored with simply watching his flock, every once in a while cried "Wolf!" in order to enjoy the resulting flurry as the men of the village rushed to what they thought was an emergency. Eventually, of course, they concluded that the boy could not be taken seriously, and when a real wolf attacked the flock, they simply ignored his alarm cries and went on with their own work.

That psychologists in their routine conduct of naturalistic experiments may be promoting just such a boy-who-cried-wolf effect is not merely idle speculation. Working in my office a few years ago, I was interrupted by a student who burst in, white faced and shaking, and asked to use the telephone to call the campus emergency number. He had just discovered a man lying face down in a pool of blood in an out-of-the-way plaza near the building where I worked. The man, we discovered later, had committed suicide by jumping off the top of a nine-story university building, and the student in my office had been among the first to discover his body. As he hurriedly dialed the phone in my office he said to me, "I would have rushed over here faster than I did—but for a minute or two as I looked at the body, *I thought it was just another psychology experiment.*"

That the conduct of social psychological field experiments should promote such hesitation to intervene in real emergencies is not only tragic, but also ironic: the event which precipitated the first research on bystander intervention was the 1964 murder of a New York City woman, Kitty Genovese. Although her cries for help and her attempts to resist her assailant were heard by no fewer than thirty-eight neighbors over a full half-hour, nobody came to her aid or even called the police. Not surprisingly, social psychologists interested in researching and overcoming real social problems such as the bystander apathy associated with the Genovese murder began experimental investigations on the factors connected with willingness to intervene in emergency situations. Yet their very research methodology, with its elaborately planned hoaxes, has had as one of its consequences the increasing danger that people will, in fact, ignore apparent emergencies on the assumption that they are "just another psychology experiment"!

The tail that wags the dog. I have tried to show that the positivistic approach in psychology, as exemplified by the use of experimentation, cannot live up to its promises concerning the predictability and control of behavior, first because of its misplaced attempt to view human beings as merely larger rats or slower computers and second because of the very limited exportability of its findings.

But even if these two criticisms did not exist, there is a third factor, clearly recognized by thoughtful critics within psychology itself, which adds further doubt regarding the usefulness of the positivistic approach. In recent years, increasing concern has been expressed about the state of *fragmentation* which exists in experimental psychology. By this I mean that there appear to be no cohesive, agreed-upon theoretical foundations upon which an edifice of experimental studies can systematically build. Instead one gets the impression that many isolated researchers are doing hundreds of scattered studies which are largely unrelated to one another. As one observer has said, "One sometimes gets the impression from the journal literature that one gets from listening to a conversation among golfers: everyone is talking, but only about his own game."[11] Another pair of critics has presented more systematic evidence for this state of fragmentation and lack of coherence: examining the contents of the prestigious *Journal of Personality and Social Psychology* over a three-year period, they found that, of over 2000 topics cited in more than 200 articles, approximately 1700 were mentioned only once; fewer than 120 were mentioned more than twice. These findings suggested to them that "only a small fraction of this field is comprised of coordinated efforts within a common conceptual framework."[12]

The reason for this state of fragmentation in psychology appears to be related to the discipline's excessive loyalty to the positivistic, and especially the experimental, approach. In doing research of any sort, it is usually expected that interest in the content of a problem will precede the choice of a methodology for its study. That is, once a topic is deemed important and worthy of research, then a search is made for the methods most suited to study it. If the chosen methodology later turns out to be faulty, a new methodology is sought or developed. But in North American psychology it very often appears that the tail is wagging the dog. In other words, the researcher's first and most unshakable commitment seems to be to the experimental method, and only after that to any given topic that might be researchable by that method. As a result, if a given topic cannot be forced somehow into an experimental design, then the chances are high that it will simply never be investigated at all. Conversely, as long as the researcher has carefully followed the six criteria for positivistic psychology, few colleagues will question the significance of whatever topic he or she has chosen to study.

It is hardly surprising that when the only thing uniting researchers has been a commitment to a common methodology, the state of psychological research has become such that "everyone is talking, but only about his [or her] own game." When the method of research so exclusively dictates the content of that research—when the tail wags the dog—such fragmentation is bound to follow. Let me emphasize again that this concern is not unique to Christians in academic psychology; it is a concern which increasingly exercises some of the most productive minds in psychology as a whole. One such critic, after many years of commitment to the experimental approach, finally wrote: "Apparently we have nothing to offer in terms of general theoretical or empirical evolutions or revolutions; nothing to discuss that would represent the basic questions or issues of our field and the paths to be taken towards their resolution."[13]

In addition, the reluctance to study any phenomenon which cannot be neatly operationalized, quantified and experimentally tested inevitably leads to a neglect of much that is uniquely human. Even the compilers of a prestigious volume entitled *Human Behavior: An Inventory of Scientific Findings* admit, after reporting 1,045 scientific findings about human behavior, that the image of humanity as it emerges from these findings is strangely incomplete:

Indeed, as one reviews this set of findings, he may well be impressed by [a] striking omission. As one lives life or observes it around him, or within himself, or finds it in a work of art, he sees a richness that has somehow fallen through the present screen of the behavioral sciences. This book, for example, has rather little to say about the central human concerns: nobility, moral courage, ethical torments, the delicate relation of father and son or of the marriage state, life's way of corrupting innocence, the rightness and wrongness of acts, evil, happiness, love and hate, death—even sex.[14]

In summary, the commitment of psychologists to positivistic research as represented by controlled experimentation falls short of its promises of predictability and control on three counts. First, it underestimates the capacity of human research participants to countermanipulate within the context of the experiment and thus to contaminate the researcher's own manipulations. Second, the exportability, or generalizability, of experimental findings—whether generated in the laboratory or the field—is severely limited. Finally, the widespread practice of studying only that which can be adapted to a purely experimental framework results in a fragmented psychology which lacks not only overall integration, but also attention to many specifically human concerns which cannot be quantified, operationalized or manipulated.

But in confining our discussion so far purely to the question of the *success* of the positivistic approach in psychology, we have not even touched upon the question of its ethical *acceptability*. It is to this latter question that we will now direct our attention.

Is the Positivistic Approach Ethically Acceptable?

Before discussing the ethics of human experimentation in psychology, we need to point out that the very phrase "ethics of experimentation" contains within itself a subtle contradiction. As we have noted previously, the very use of the experimental method assumes that the materials being manipulated in the experiment—for example, the iron filings of the physicist or the frogs of the physiologist—are unreflective, unfree respondents to inexorable laws of nature which it is the scientist's task to uncover by experimentation. Furthermore, since iron filings and frogs are assumed to be unreflective and unfree, they are also assumed to be morally neutral: we do not praise and reward frogs for behaving well, nor do we punish or imprison them for failing to do what we want, because only free, reflective beings who are capable of real choices can be held morally accountable for those choices. By extension, then, the use of human beings in psychology experiments must presuppose—consciously or unconsciously—that they, like the iron filings and the frogs, are also unfree, unreflective respondents to natural laws which they cannot transcend. As such, they cannot, any more than the frog, ever be held ethically accountable for anything they do.

But by this reasoning, the human researchers who conduct psychology experiments must themselves share these characteristics of unfreedom and unreflectiveness; consequently, they too cannot be held morally accountable for any of their actions —including their experimental activities—since all such actions have presumably been caused by some natural law and are not the result of their own free choices. Yet, in the field of academic psychology, most of these same human researchers do not presume themselves to be amoral robots, but in fact do think about and talk about the rightness and wrongness of their own experimental activities.

We can be grateful that they do—grateful that they themselves do not behave in a way consistent with their own positivistic model of human beings as unfree and therefore morally unaccountable. For if they were completely consistent with that approach, there would be no reason for them not to experiment with human beings in any way whatsoever, not even short of the kinds of atrocities performed in Nazi concentration camps, since they could not, as unfree beings themselves, ever be blamed for anything they did. The fact that psychologists experimenting with human beings do, in fact, engage in moral self-scrutiny regarding their own experimental activity in no way makes them any more logically consistent: it merely means that "as men, they are better than their theories."[15]

Stress and deception.   What then are the features of psychology experiments which prompt ethical concern? Briefly, they are the inflicting of *stress* (in some experiments) and the use of *deception* (in a high percentage of experiments). Let us first be clear that the stress inflicted on participants in psychology experiments is rarely physical, although it may (as in the Schacter experiment) involve the temporary anticipation of physical stress which is not in fact forthcoming. Let us also be clear that any deception practiced by researchers is always dealt with in the postexperimental debriefing session, when the participants are told the true purpose of the study, and researchers admit and excuse themselves for any deceptions used. But in the absence of clear guidelines as to what constitutes acceptable levels of stress and deception, there have been a number of experiments undertaken which, once publicized, have prompted concern. A brief description of some of the more famous stress and deception experiments follows:

1. An experimenter at Stanford University explains to participants that he is investigating homosexual arousal. He tells them that as they watch pictures of men flashed on a screen, changes in their skin conductivity as shown on a dial will indicate the extent of their homosexual inclinations. As the students watch the slides, they observe to their dismay that the needle on the dial does a lot of jumping. In actual fact, the jumping of the needle was contrived by the experimenter, whose real interest was not in homosexual arousal but rather in the extent to which people who discover they have an undesirable trait tend to project that trait onto others.

2. In an Ohio State University study, an experimenter wishes to find out whether people who feel guilty are likely to perform a favor for the person they have wronged. On the pretext of doing research for his M.A. thesis on motor learning, he seats subjects before an elaborate machine with many buttons and switches. As he instructs them in its use, he also

warns them to be very careful with it, since all his research money is tied up in the equipment. As the student cautiously pushes buttons on the machine, a dramatic, noisy breakdown of the equipment is simulated. The experimenter pretends extreme distress, weeping that now he will never get his master's degree. Before the apologetic student leaves the laboratory, the experimenter casually asks if he will sign a (preposterous) petition supporting university tuition increases. Fifty-six percent of the guilt-stricken students do, in fact, sign.

3. Another Stanford University researcher wonders whether a young woman's level of self-esteem affects her propensity to fall in love. A suave and handsome male graduate student is recruited as an accomplice to the experimenter, and, posing as a fellow student waiting to participate in another experiment, he strikes up a conversation with arriving female participants one by one, eventually making a date with each. Next, in a private interview with the experimenter, half of these women are told, supposedly on the basis of personality tests taken a week earlier, that they have very attractive personality profiles, while the other half are told that they have "basically immature drives," a "weak personality," "a lack of flexibility and originality" and "a lack of capacity for successful leadership." Finally, the women are asked to rate their liking for certain persons, including a teacher, a friend and "since we have one space left, why don't you also rate that fellow from Miss Turner's study whom you were waiting with?" The result: the women with lowered self-esteem (the ones given the negative personality assessment) tended to report liking the handsome graduate student more than those whose self-esteem had been raised by a positive personality report.

4. A Yale University psychologist wishes to investigate social conditions which promote unquestioning obedience to authority. A stooge (in fact, a professional actor) is engaged to pose as a fellow participant with each arriving, naive sub-

ject, and both are told that they are taking part in a study on the effects of punishment on learning efficiency. The stooge is to be the "learner" and, locked in a cubicle with electrodes strapped to his arm, he is told that the other participant (the naive subject) will be coaching him as he learns a list of word pairs. The naive subject is then led to an elaborate-looking shock generator and told that each time the "learner" makes a mistake, he is to give him a brief electric shock, increasing the voltage with each mistake made. As the stooge makes frequent preprogrammed errors, the naive subject, at the experimenter's continued urging, administers what he thinks to be progressively higher-level shocks. (In fact, the shock generator does not give shocks at all.) The stooge protests and screams convincingly as the "shock" level increases, while the experimenter keeps telling the uneasy subject that "the experiment must continue." Only a small percentage of the naive subjects defy the experimenter and refuse to go on "shocking" the learner.[16]

Let it be admitted at the outset that these four studies are among the most extreme in their use of stress and deception. The false arousal of homosexual anxiety, guilt, low self-esteem, or meek submission to authority is fortunately not a daily practice in North American psychology. But the routine use of deception and the infliction of some sort of temporary distress has been common enough to prompt an ongoing debate in psychology literature. "Countless experiments," writes one follower of this debate, "can be cited in which subjects have received (or administered) electric shock, received fictitious or true reports of inadequacy on intelligence or personality tests, failed at a task, been exposed to the sight or sound of another in distress, (or) been insulted or related harshly to by the experimenter or his accomplice."[17] In addition, the practice of deception in North American psychology experiments has become more and more routine. A review done at the beginning of the 1970s found the incidence of deception in the areas of personality and social psychology to be around forty per cent, with some specific research problems (for example, research on conformity) using deception close to one hundred per cent of the time.[18]

According to what principles are such practices defended? Two arguments are continually invoked. The first holds that any stress inflicted is very temporary, since participants are always debriefed (reassured and told the true purpose of the study) as soon as their responses to the experimental manipulations have been recorded. The second argument holds, in effect, that the end justifies the means—that is, that what is learned about human nature and behavior in such experiments necessitates and excuses the use of both stress and deception. Let us examine each of these arguments in turn.

Some not-so-temporary aftereffects. It is by no means certain, in the absence of extensive follow-up, that a hasty debriefing effectively erases any psychological unease invoked during the experiment itself. One critic argues that most volunteers for experiments—even among the student population—are unaware of the distinction between research and clinical psychologists, and come to the experiment privately "seeking an opportunity to have contact with, be noticed by, and perhaps confide in a person with psychological training."[19] This attitude of trusting dependence on the experimenter is deepened all the more by the participant's unfamiliarity with the laboratory situation, its demands and its technical trappings. Consequently, the truly naive subject is unusually vulnerable and prepared to believe what he or she is told.

When the experimenter elaborately convinces a participant that he is homosexual, then later dismisses the whole scenario as a ruse perpetrated in the name of science, three effects may remain. Within the context of the immediate experiment, there is no good reason why the researcher, who admits to having lied so blithely during the experiment itself, should suddenly be believed during the debriefing. In fact, there are not a few experiments which have employed what is known as "higher-order deception": that is, the participants are falsely debriefed after one part of the experiment in order to prepare them for a second manipulation, and only after their responses to this second manipulation have been recorded are they told the purpose of the entire study. The participant may well leave the laboratory not knowing what to believe ("Do I, or do I not, have homosexual tendencies?") with the result that the psychological doubts with which he first entered the situation are simply deepened. Second, the mistrust and disillusionment generated by the researcher's double talk may later generalize to a clinical psychologist in a counseling situation, where trust is a crucial ingredient in the therapeutic process.

Third, the results of stress and deception in the psychological laboratory have potential repercussions beyond the experiment itself and the later lives of its participants. For as prominent academics in the social sciences continue to practice lying for a good cause, they become, by virtue of their prestige and status, role models for the belief that routine deception is justified in the name of any good cause. We have already had ample evidence of such an attitude in highly placed people connected with the U.S. Watergate conspiracy and the Canadian Mounted Police investigations, both products of loyalty to "the party" or "the nation's safety." It is indeed ironic that psychologists, seventy per cent of whom label themselves as politically left of center,[20] are inclined to condemn such behavior in government circles without seeing in it any similarity to their own professional behavior or taking any responsibility for fostering a readiness in others to let the end justify the means. Yet the end result of routine deception in both arenas is the same—a rapid escalation of mistrust and cynicism on the part of the ordinary person toward some of the very institutions (namely, the university and the government) previously thought to be the mainsprings of a cooperative society.

Nor are ethical problems diminished by a greater use of naturalistic experimentation, such as that represented by the mock faintings in the New York subway. Indeed, as the experimental psychologist leaves the laboratory and enters the public space, a whole host of new legal questions arises. In such naturalistic research blatant deception is eliminated, and subjects, unaware that they are in an experiment, are spared any feelings of violated trust. But on the other hand, participants who are not aware of their experimental role cannot give their informed consent to play that role, nor can they in most cases be tracked down later to receive an explanation and clarification of the research itself.[21] In addition, given the highly dramatic nature of many field experiments, one wonders who would be legally responsible if a fragile bystander, confronted with a mock fainting, mugging or street fight, succumbed to a real heart attack and collapsed.[22]

Do the ends justify the means? It is not as if psychologists in North America have not struggled to come up with a solution to the problems posed by the use of stress, and especially deception, in experimental research with human beings. The official stance of the American Psychological Association (A.P.A.) regarding the use of deception is what the organization terms a "cost/benefits" approach.[23] According to this rule of thumb, individual researchers, when contemplating the possibility of using deception in an experimental design, must ask themselves whether the benefits of the resultant findings are likely to outweigh the costs of having to deceive those who will be participating in the experiment. This is just another way of saying that they are enjoined to explain why the ends of their research justify the means used to arrive at those ends. Of course, ends or benefits can be defined with reference to many standards, but the A.P.A. generally understands the terms to refer to the benefits of knowledge gained about human nature and behavior as a result of experimental research; if such knowledge is both important and reliable, then, it is argued, the use of deception during the research process can surely be justified.

But if this is the criterion to be used, then it can certainly be argued that the ends rarely justify the means, since the amount of really significant and usable knowledge about human beings to be derived from psychology experiments is slight. We have already shown that the use of deception in such experiments breeds, in the long run, suspicion on the part of more and more experimental participants before they even enter the laboratory, thus making it highly uncertain that they will react to the experimenter's manipulations in a naive and uncalculated fashion. We have also shown that findings based on psychology experiments, which are the chief vehicles for the use of deception, also have limited usefulness because of the unrepresentative nature of the times, persons and settings connected with such experiments, and because of their tendency to focus on fragmented, isolated aspects of human behavior rather than on the whole person in an ongoing context of time and space.

In addition, further research strongly suggests that findings from such laboratory experiments are suspect for yet another reason: the very presence of the experimenter may influence the participants to respond in the way that the experimenter hopes or wishes them to. In other words, the results that the experimenter obtains may sometimes be due not to the experimental manipulations objectively and impersonally imposed, but to the experimenter's own personal desires regarding the outcome of the study. Harvard social scientist Robert Rosenthal has both conducted and surveyed research which suggests that such self-fulfilling prophecies in psychological research are too common to be ignored.[24] He has also presented evidence which suggests that the objective purity of experimental manipulations can be affected by additional "experimenter effects" formerly thought to be totally irrelevant to the outcome of the study—factors such as the experimenter's race, sex, religion and personality.[25] To the extent that these effects exist, they further undermine the claim that the knowledge gained through the use of deception-laden experiments is sufficiently reliable to justify the routine use of such deception.

The real beneficiaries of psychology experiments. There are still other problems with the A.P.A.'s cost/benefits strategy for making a decision about the use of deception in psychology experiments. First, the individual researcher is said to have satisfied the professional code as long as he or she has engaged in the mere exercise of weighing costs against benefits, regardless of the decision finally made. But such an approach totally fails to separate ethical from unethical practices; it merely states that the researcher is behaving ethically as long as he or she has engaged in the cognitive process of thinking about costs and benefits. Such an exercise is unlikely to reduce the use of deception because the final decision does not need to be appealed to anyone else, such as a group of uninvolved colleagues or of representatives for experimental participants. Since the researcher is usually habituated to using and idealizing the approach represented by the experimental method, he or she is probably not highly motivated to look for other approaches to studying the problem. Consequently, it can be argued, he or she has a strongly vested interest in continuing to rationalize the use of deception.

Finally, it is never made totally clear in the A.P.A. ethics manuals whose costs and whose benefits are to be weighed in the equation when deciding on the use of deception. Both costs and benefits can be considered from the point of view of the participant, the experimenter or society at large; furthermore, costs and benefits can be both immediate and long-term. Various critics have argued that neither research participants nor the larger society have yet benefited in any significant way from the isolated, contrived scenarios staged in psychology laboratories. Indeed, one critic has gone so far as to accuse experimental psychologists involved in social and personality research of being "laboratory exhibitionists," more concerned to see how cleverly they can hoodwink their subjects and impress their colleagues with neat operationalizations than they are to increase understanding of human behavior or to serve the public good.[26] By a process of elimination, then, it appears to be the experimenter's own advancement in a restricted professional circle that is the major, if not the sole, beneficiary of the use of deception in laboratory experiments.

Yet there are certain others, outside the profession, who stand to benefit from the experimental approach to human behavior. In spite of all the limitations detailed above, there are still practical uses for the kinds of "probabilistic generalizations" arising from laboratory and field experiments involving human beings. In a technological, Western society such as our own, human beings are consumers and voters, and as such they are the frequent targets of experiments in both advertising and political campaigning. In each of these endeavors, success (in terms of gaining sales or gaining political office) does not depend on being able to predict and control the responses of every single person who is exposed to a persuasive message. Rather, success is achieved as long as your product has more buyers than your competitor's, or your candidate more votes than his or her opponent. In doing experiments aimed at predicting the behavior of either consumers or voters, one can tolerate individual differences arising from cynicism or suspicion; one can also tolerate limitations on the generalizability of one's findings; one can even tolerate a substantial percentage of casualties— people who believed the message and bought a product which later turned out to be bad for them, such as a soap which prompts an allergic reaction among a minority of users. As long as the total number of persons buying the product or voting for the candidate exceeds that of the competition, there is no need for predictability and control down to the level of the individual.

It seems then that psychology's positivistic, experimental approach to people is of great benefit to those in business and politics; indeed, some historians of twentieth-century American psychology have argued that psychology has always been primarily the servant of business, industry and politics, despite any rhetoric about "knowledge for knowledge's sake," and that this is precisely why the experimental method has been so single-mindedly adhered to.[27] Yet, from a Christian standpoint, there is much to be concerned about in this. When people are approached primarily as potential product buyers or vote casters, with a view to getting as many as possible to respond to the manipulation of an advertisement or a campaign message, a profound dehumanization takes place. The businessman or politician all too easily forgets to ask whether the "product" being sold is in the best interests of the individual consumer or voter, and all too easily begins to think only in terms of how mass human responses can be most effectively manipulated for a single, isolated purpose at a single, isolated point in time. The same attitude can also lead to what some social critics have called "majoritarianism"—that is, a preoccupation with whatever works (in terms of generating sales or votes) for the greatest number of people, with the concerns of any leftover minority groups treated as mere deviations or error variance in the data.

It can be argued that the experimental tradition in North American psychology has both influenced and been influenced by the manipulative majoritarianism which characterizes all too much of the activity of business, industry and politics. As early as 1913, applied psychologist Hugo Muensterberg in a volume entitled *Psychology and Industrial Efficiency*, wrote, "Our aim is to sketch the outlines of a new science which is to be intermediate between the modern psychology laboratory and the problems of economics: the psychological experiment is systematically to be placed at the service of commerce and industry." Moreover, according to Muensterberg, psychologists were to proffer only their methodological skills and not their opinions as to how these techniques ought or ought not to be used, for

> while the psychologists have to perform the actual labor, the representatives of practical life are much better able to indicate the points at which the psychological levers ought to be employed.... Economic psychotechnics may serve certain

ends of commerce and industry, but whether these ends are the best ones is not a case with which the psychologist has to be burdened. The psychologist is, therefore, not entangled in the economic discussions of the day; it is not his concern to decide whether the policy of the trusts or the policy of the trade unions or any other policy is the ideal one. He is confined to the statement: If you wish this end, then you must proceed in this way.[28]

Thus, right from the early days of North American psychology, there have been pressures on psychologists to be mere technicians and to apply their research skills to the accomplishment of ends which would be determined by the representatives of practical life. And while psychologists in succeeding decades have both urged and demonstrated greater moral and social concern, there is a strange and awkward contradiction in their very attempts to do so, because, as we pointed out earlier, their very research approach is one which works on the assumption that human actions are mechanistically determined and therefore morally nonaccountable. But how can psychologists, faced with ethical decisions regarding the use of their powers, consistently view themselves as amoral machines? Yet where, in a research career which constantly calls them to think and produce in mechanistic, amoral terms about human behavior, are psychologists to gain the insight to make such moral decisions?

At the very least, such a contradiction, between the human being as amoral machine or animal and the human being as at least to some degree free and therefore morally accountable, must breed a profound schizophrenia in the lives of those who must live with it. To the extent that it does, it is doubtful how much even experimental psychologists themselves benefit from their own research. Of course there are many psychologists, not a few of whom are professing Christians, who claim to avoid this contradiction by stating that the mechanistic model of humanity is merely a research metaphor for use in exploring one limited aspect of persons, mindful always that there is much more to them in the realms of freedom and creativity that can just as validly be explored by other means. But given the overwhelming research attention and resources devoted to this one mechanistic aspect of human functioning, such an admission of the need for other nonexperimental, nonmechanistic approaches becomes a case of "damning with faint praise": it is a superficial concession to the need for alternative approaches which is virtually never accompanied by any efforts to support or develop them.

In addition, we are always in danger of being seduced by the metaphors with which we work day after day and year after year. Many psychologists may feel that as long as they privately, and perhaps publicly, acknowledge the limitations of their natural-scientific approach, they can continue to use this approach in their working lives without personal hazard to themselves. But evidence that this may not be the case comes from one of the heroes of North American psychology. Charles Darwin, at the end of a lifetime's work developing the theory of evolutionistic continuity between animals and humans, wrote with great regret that "my mind seems to have become a kind of machine for grinding general laws out of large collections of facts," one result of which was a "curious and lamentable loss of the higher aesthetic tastes":

> Up to the age of thirty, or beyond it, poetry of many kinds ... gave me great pleasure, and even as a schoolboy I took intense delight in Shakespeare, especially in the historical plays. I have also said that formerly pictures gave me considerable, and music very great delight. But now for many years I cannot endure to read a line of poetry; I have tried lately to read Shakespeare and found it so intolerably dull that it nauseated me. I have also lost almost any taste for pictures or music.... The loss of these tastes is a loss of happiness, and may possibly be injurious to the intellect, and more probably to the moral character by enfeebling the emotional part of our nature.[29]

Darwin penned these warnings to would-be scientists in the latter part of the nineteenth century. Almost a hundred years later, American methodologist David Bakan, commenting on the state of psychology's apprenticeship to the natural sciences, recalled a psychology student who decided to leave school completely rather than risk the loss of which Darwin spoke.

> Not too long ago a very able graduate student told me that he had decided to leave school, and that he no longer wanted to be a psychologist. I was very much taken aback by this. He was bright, doing well, and receiving a good stipend. In the course of the conversation he made one remark which spoke of his deep feelings about psychology. He told me that he did not want to become a "hollow man," and that if he stayed he was afraid he might become one. As he spoke ... it occurred to me that ["hollow men"] may well be a metaphorical projection of the state into which we are trying to discipline our young psychologists.[30]

The Apprenticeship Unfulfilled

Neither Darwin nor the perceptive psychology student of whom Bakan wrote remained personally satisfied with their apprenticeship in the natural-scientific approach to humanity. But much of this chapter has tried to demonstrate, not that the apprenticeship of psychology to natural science is personally unsatisfying, but simply that it does not work. We began this chapter with the thesis that if the six criteria of positivistic science are strictly enforced in psychology, then the research which is faithful to all six criteria—namely, experimental psychology—must yield an especially thorough and reliable understanding of human psychological processes. We then proceeded to illustrate how the results of psychology experiments using human participants are subject to a great many limitations in terms of their reliability and exportability, thus raising the question of whether experimental research should continue as the preferred method for studying human behavior.

More than one critic from within the profession now believes that it should not. One has expressed it in this manner:

There may be a useful role for experiments in social psychology, but it will be a *supplementary* role. Within our present norms, the investigator who does not manipulate independent variables is impelled to offer an extra measure of justification for his procedure, or at least [to explain] how his studies can lead to experiments. The converse should apply. The experiment should be regarded as the atypical endeavor and experimenters should be required to provide special justification in light of the special problems and limitations inherent in the method.[31]

But if the experiment is to become an atypical endeavor in psychology, rather than its typical method, what is to replace it? And if the mechanistic approach to human beings is as self-defeating as I have tried to show, what alternative visions are possible? These questions are the principal concerns of chapter three.

CHAPTER 3

THE APPRENTICE IN SEARCH OF A NEW MASTER

LET US BRIEFLY REVIEW the terrain we have traveled to this point. Chapter one argued that the natural-scientific enterprise generally, and North American psychology particularly, developed in a context of increasing secularism, self-confident rationalism, and technologism. By applying the suffix *-ism* to these trends, I am suggesting that they constitute a species of "hidden agenda" or ideology behind the touted neutrality and objectivity of the scientific method—one which persists to this day, and which it is naive for any scholar, Christian or otherwise, to ignore. Chapter two made an internal critique of the natural-science approach in psychology. It intended to show that psychology's use of a technological metaphor to study human beings (approaching them primarily as "larger rats or slower computers") results in both methodological and ethical contradictions which are at the heart of psychology's current identity crisis.

This final chapter asks, Where might we go from here? What are the possibilities for a new master to whom psychology might apprentice itself? Exploring that question will constitute a major part of this chapter; but as a prelude to that exercise, two further questions need consideration. First, why is it important to look at such alternatives now? Second, to whom is the original question addressed? We will deal with these preliminary issues in the order given.

A Period of Extraordinary Science

We detailed in the last chapter the methodological and ethical contradictions which have been developing in positivistic academic psychology. We also mentioned the growing sense of fragmentation that has especially afflicted the areas of psychology (such as personality and social psychology) which continue to use methods developed on subhuman entities to study complex individual and interpersonal functions. Taken together, these problems suggest that psychology may be on the brink of a period of *extraordinary science*. This is a term coined by Thomas Kuhn, a theoretical physicist turned historian of science, in his landmark volume *The Structure of Scientific Revolutions*.[1]

Kuhn's book perhaps more than any other has been instrumental in questioning the notion that the practice of science is a kind of disembodied, metaphysical ideal to which all practitioners adhere at all times. In contrast to this Neo-Platonic view of science, Kuhn introduced the idea of *paradigms*, which he defined in at least two senses. Paradigms can be, first, the disciplinary matrix of metaphysical, theoretical and methodological commitments shared by the members of the field. They also include, second, the "universally recognized scientific achievements that for a time provide model problems and solutions to a community of practitioners."[2] In what Kuhn called *periods of normal science*, there is generally a single paradigm that unites all practitioners. In other words, certain key concepts are accepted by the entire disciplinary community, and it is this shared corpus of presuppositions, in both senses of the term *paradigm*, that concerns us here.

While paradigms are not totally static or rigid, neither are they infinitely flexible. For when an anomaly, or violation of paradigmatic expectation, occurs, there is an attempt to make it conform to the existing paradigm in some way. In addition, Kuhn suggests, the stability of the ruling paradigm is assured by the way in which newcomers to the discipline are assimilated: rarely are students introduced to a science at its highest level of abstraction or by a consideration of its most controversial foundational questions. Rather, they undergo an apprenticeship by being introduced to exemplary experiments or studies and then being urged to apply the same idealized approach to a problem of their own.

Kuhn takes pains to point out that as long as a given paradigm dominates a scientific discipline, it generates a sense of unity, common purpose and inevitable progress. This is the state of affairs during what Kuhn calls periods of normal science. During such a stage, even when major problems challenge the paradigm, there is pressure to continue operating within it as long as possible. Only when an anomaly becomes so glaring that it clearly resists incorporation into the existing paradigm is there what Kuhn calls a *paradigm shift*. Between the crisis in the old paradigm and that paradigm's replacement by another comes what Kuhn calls the stage of *extraordinary science*. It is a limbo state during which the habit of appealing to accepted theories and approaches begins to break down, precisely because it is becoming evident that the old approaches are not as adequate and all-encompassing as formerly believed. Kuhn describes the stage of extraordinary science in these terms:

Confronted with anomaly or with crisis, scientists take a different attitude toward existing paradigms, and the nature of their research changes accordingly. The proliferation of competing articulations, the willingness to try anything, the expression of explicit discontent, the recourse to philosophy and to debate over fundamentals—all these are symptoms of a transition from normal to extraordinary research.[3]

Now, in light of what has been discussed in the previous chapter, I would submit that present-day psychology, as an academic discipline, is teetering on the brink of a period of extraordinary science. It is confronted by anomalies which, despite heroic efforts, it cannot incorporate into its existing natural-science-based paradigm. The essence of the previous chapter was a discussion of what I take to be the most important, obvious and increasingly debated of these anomalies—namely, the failure of the experimental method to overcome human reflexivity and the inability of that same mechanistic approach to generate from within itself a moral code for its own regulation.

There are indications in psychology that these strains in the paradigmatic edifice have already begun to be felt. For example, some of the best indicators of the past dominance of the natural-science paradigm can be seen in the introductory texts by means of which students have been socialized into the discipline. Excerpts from the opening chapters of four texts written before the mid-1970s reveal just how entrenched this paradigm has been:

The distinguishing feature of psychology is that it observes and attempts to understand the behavior of organisms.

Psychology is the science of human and animal behavior.

Psychology is the science that seeks to measure, explain, and change behavior.

Psychology is the science that seeks to describe and explain and, on occasion, to change the behavior of man and other animals.[4]

However, in the more recently written best-selling texts, there are indications that this view of psychology is loosening up. Thus, the seventh edition of Hilgard, Atkinson and Atkinson's much used *Introduction to Psychology* titles its first section "Psychology as a Scientific and Humanistic Endeavor" and then goes on to define psychology as "the science that studies behavior *and* mental processes." It tells the student that psychological research embraces several approaches—for example, neurobiological, behavioral, cognitive, psychoanalytic, phenomenological and humanistic—and that the approach to a given problem need not be limited to any single one of these. At the same time, however, the text goes on to state that "when applicable, the experimental method is preferred for studying problems because it seeks to control all variables except the one being studied, and provides for precise measurement of the independent and dependent variables."[5]

The foregoing is a striking example of the attitude within psychology which I have called "teetering on the brink of extraordinary science": the ruling natural-science paradigm is still given pride of place, but there is also clear evidence of the "proliferation of competing articulations" that Kuhn has designated as one of the signs of a shift from normal to extraordinary science. Other indicators are equally striking. For instance, persons embarking on an undergraduate career in psychology have always been told that, regardless of their ultimately desired specialty (even if it is clinical or counseling psychology) they must still take, and excel in, courses in experimental design and statistical analysis. In addition, they must show that they can apply these skills in the conduct of a piece of independent research in their graduating year—a kind of minithesis to give them a taste of what graduate school requirements are like. Although this is still largely the ruling standard, it is worth noting that in 1971 for the first time the American Psychological Association allowed a student to write a nonempirical doctoral thesis in one of its accredited graduate programs.[6] In addition, although (as we have seen) psychology began as an official discipline by self-consciously severing its background ties to philosophy, there is a growing movement to bring the two back into a mutually influential dialog. An example of this is the formation in 1975 of the Society for Philosophy and Psychology. Such events would appear to reflect the "recourse to philosophy" by which Kuhn also characterized a shift to extraordinary science.

Now in one sense it is anything but comfortable to practice one's profession during a period when it is beginning to question its moorings. During periods of normal science, everything is much more straightforward: training procedures are largely standardized; there is a direct relationship between that training and how one goes on to do research and, in turn, train others; the criteria for what constitutes "worthy" and "rigorous" research are generally agreed upon and uniformly enforced. When disputes do occur, they are about the details, rather than the substance or fundamental approach, of the discipline. In short, academic life is in many ways smoother and more predictable for both students and professors. It is, however, also more totalitarian. On one level, the student or professor is bound by explicit norms concerning what constitutes a scientific law or concept in the field. Such statements tend to define the boundaries both of acceptable research problems *and* acceptable solutions. On another level, there is a set of commitments to preferred methods and instruments and to the ways in which they may be employed. And on a still deeper level, there are what Kuhn calls "quasi-metaphysical commitments" which in effect tell the scientist what sorts of entities and relationships the universe does and does not contain.[7]

I have tried to show in chapters one and two that North American psychology's paradigm has been characterized by a metaphysical commitment to evolutionism as a world view as well as to positivism as a methodology. Those who have been uncomfortable with either aspect of this paradigm were at best relegated to the fringes of the discipline or at worst ostracized from it completely. But all of this, as we have seen, is beginning to change, with the result that yesterday's marginal members of the psychology community may be on their way to becoming tomorrow's role models. In such a climate the place of the Christian student, professor or practitioner of psychology becomes potentially crucial. This leads me to my second introductory question—to whom is the original question (Where might we go from here?) addressed?

Some Christian Approaches to the Mechanistic/Personalistic Dilemma

Up to this point in my writing, my imaginary audience has not been exclusively Christian. It is true that I have touched upon some concerns which may be of interest to Christians in particular—concerns such as secularization, research ethics and atheism among social scientists. But the major points to which I have addressed myself are already developed areas of concern among many mainstream psychologists; indeed, my supporting evidence over the past two chapters has been drawn largely from secular, not Christian, sources in psychology. Now, however, I want to address myself particularly, rather than just inclusively, to psychology students, professionals and concerned observers who are confessing Christians. My reason for doing so is both embarrassing and puzzling: Christian psychologists, far from being vanguard critics of psychology's overweening positivism, have generally been among its strongest defenders. I want now to document the accuracy of this characterization and to suggest some possible reasons for such a situation before considering possible directions for reform with which Christians in psychology might be comfortable.

To document the Christian alliance with positivism, I will turn my attention to a recent work which summarizes some directions in social science generally and in its Christian expression particularly, philosopher Stephen Evans's book *Preserving the Person: A Look at the Human Sciences*. As implied by its title, this work takes on one of the questions with which I have been grappling—namely, whether the essentially mechanistic image of persons which emerges from the behavioral sciences (by which Evans means brain physiology, psychology and sociology) is at all reconcilable with the traditional and biblical view that human beings can at least partially transcend environmental determinants and therefore be capable of creativity and also morally accountable for actions performed. Evans refers to this as the "mechanistic/personalistic dilemma." He is neither uncritically scientific nor defensively antiscientific in his consideration of this problem. He freely acknowledges some of the strengths and uses of the mechanistic model of persons. He also reminds readers that "the fact that the acceptance of a scientific view of man would be painful is no argument against it. . . . To the extent that these scientists offer us truth about the human condition, nothing will be gained by denying or ignoring that truth."[8] But he also shows, as I myself have tried to do in a more specialized manner, how the espousal of a purely mechanistic view of humanity leads to inescapable anomalies or self-contradictions.

But Evans's particular contribution, for our present purposes, is his very useful typology of the various ways in which Christians have coped with the tensions of this mechanistic/personalistic dilemma. More specifically, he delineates three broad ways (each of which subdivides in two) that have been used to reconcile the mechanistic, natural-science view of persons with the biblical image of human beings as creative, rational and accountable. Evans acknowledges that some of the Christian thinkers he cites cannot be reduced to pure types, falling into one exclusive category or another. Nevertheless, these categories are very useful for developing a historical and logical understanding of this question.

Evans suggests that some Christians may cope with the mechanistic/personalistic dilemma by reinterpreting the traditional, biblical view of persons in accordance with their desire to believe that the natural-science account is both ultimate and complete. Some may go so far as to capitulate to a totally mechanistic view and justify it by leaning heavily and one-sidedly on those passages of Scripture which emphasize the sovereignty of God. "[The *Capitulators*] will claim that nowhere does the Bible

---

Evans's Routes to Resolution

---

1. Reinterpreters	2. Limiters	3. Humanizers
of the Person	of Science	of Science
a. Compatibilists	*a. Territorialists*	*a. Particularists*
b. Capitulators	*b. Perspectivalists*	*b. Generalists*

---

clearly teach any philosophical doctrine of 'free will.' Rather the Bible pictures a God who controls and determines all things for his own purposes. ... The mechanical laws which the scientist discovers are simply interpreted by the Capitulator as the *means* whereby God's sovereign decrees are accomplished." Nevertheless, says Evans, the truly consistent Capitulator is a rare bird among Christians, simply because anyone with a high view of Scripture must also account for its many exhortations from God and his messengers to choose rightly and refrain from evil. "Such exhortations hardly make sense in a context where human beings do not have *any* freedom to make decisions. If all human beings inevitably do the will of God, then what sense can be made of a God who pleads with his people to turn from sin to himself?"[9]

It is because of such problems that, historically, most Christian Reinterpreters of the Person have been what Evans calls *Compatibilists* rather than Capitulators. Compatibilists (whom Evans also calls "soft determinists") try to have the best of both worlds. They say, in effect, that human beings are both free and determined in a way too mysterious to be grasped by merely human understanding, a position which Evans maintains is neither lazy nor equivocal, provided it is the result of a reasoned intellectual struggle. This position has historically been quite typical of Calvinist theologians, who maintained in the Westminster Confession, for example, that "although in relation to the foreknowledge and decree of God, the first cause, all things come to pass immutably and infallibly, yet by the same providence he ordereth them to fall out, according to the nature of second causes, either necessarily, freely, or contingently."[10]

Although there are still persistent philosophical problems with this Compatibilist position, Evans states (and I agree) that its ongoing support by many careful Christian thinkers warrants its continued consideration. Nevertheless, he concludes, no Christian can really be a pure Reinterpreter of either the Capitulator or Compatibilist type. A pure Reinterpreter, by Evans's philosophy-of-science-based definition, is someone who holds that natural-scientific truth is both exhaustive and ultimate, but a truly Christian Reinterpreter "will . . . insist that the scientific story is *not* the whole story. Science [may] give us an account of the *how* of God's doings, the *means* whereby God's decrees are accomplished. But science cannot tell us the *why*; God's purposes in ordering the universe as he does are opaque to the scientist. The meaning of an act is not exhausted by the mechanical account."[11] This means that most Christian Reinterpreters are really on their way to joining Evans's second broad type, which he calls the *Limiters of Science*. This is the category into which, in fact, most evangelical psychologists in North America (and Britain) fall. Consequently it deserves careful attention.

Limiters of Science are also of two types, according to Evans. The first kind, whom Evans labels *Territorialists*, represent a position which for many years—yea, centuries—was the establishment position of the church. Territorialists are essentially Cartesian dualists, who see human beings as a body plus an ephemeral something else: mind, soul, spirit. They acknowledge the right of science to investigate and declare mechanical the workings of man's physical side, but the mental or spiritual aspects they claim to be impenetrable by the scientific method and strictly off limits to working scientists. As we saw in chapter one, it is likely that this was the view of many prescientific "psychologists" in North America. Before the late nineteenth century, as we have seen, anything approximating what we now call psychology was the province of theologians, pastors and church educators, and did not involve specific natural-science training at all, presumably because it was believed that only religious specialists could adequately deal with the higher processes reflective of the image of God in man. This kind of dualism is totally absent from North American psychology today, but it is still a live option among certain thinkers (both Christian and non-Christian) in other fields. One of the most perceptive dualistic (or territorial) thinkers is probably the Catholic physicist and historian of science Stanley L. Jaki, whose book *Brain, Mind, and Computers* is a scholarly and persuasive argument for the inappropriateness of a purely physical model of the mind.[12] Indeed, it is not uncommon for even highly specialized brain scientists to become dualists as a result of constantly uncovering more questions than answers in their attempts to relate brain processes to thinking functions. Two famous examples are Sir John Eccles, the British neurophysiologist, and Wilder Penfield, a neurosurgeon renowned for his clinical work on the relationship of brain functions to epilepsy and other disorders.[13]

Perspectivalism: A Common Christian Approach

Among Protestant evangelicals, however, the Limiters of Science are generally not Evans's Territorialists, but rather what he calls *Perspectivalists*. Perspectivalists differ from Territorialists in arguing that the natural-scientific method can be used to study the nonphysical side of human beings. The results of such an approach, they admit, may be (indeed, will be) partial or incomplete, but it is still capable of delivering some aspects of truth about human functioning. The names of Malcolm Jeeves and Donald MacKay (a psychologist and a brain scientist respectively) are so clearly associated with this point of view as to be almost household names among evangelical scientists and social scientists. MacKay summarizes the Perspectivalist position very neatly when he declares:

No part of this world of observable events is outside the boundary of scientific study. However little the scientist may make
of some of these from his professional standpoint, he is certainly entitled to try. His conclusions, however limited in
scope, may be of real help in appropriate circumstances.[14]

Having thus both rescued and relativized the natural-scientific
approach to studying persons, MacKay goes on to tell the reader
that often a given event may be completely understood only in
terms of two or more "complementary perspectives" (hence the
name *Perspectivalist*), only one of which will be that of the natural scientist. His repeated metaphor is that of an electric signboard: from the electrician's perspective, an exhaustive account
of it can be given in terms of wires, amperes, kilowatts, resis-
tances and so forth. But such an account, while exhaustive according to its own perspective, has nothing to do with what the
sign actually says—that is to say, with its meaning or significance as an economic, psychological, literary or even religious
phenomenon. To explore any of these other perspectives, we
must begin our analysis of the signboard anew in the appropriate
(and often nonscientific) language of economics, literary criticism or biblical revelation:

The advertisement is not something left over on the board if
we take away all the items of the electrician's list. It is rather
the point or significance of what is there—something we find
by starting all over again and describing the same situation
in different, but equally justifiable and illuminating categories. If you come to the board prepared to describe it only
in electrical terms you will see nothing but lamps and wires.
If you come to the very same board with a different state of
readiness, prepared to *read* it, you will see the advertisement.
There is nothing optional or arbitrary about this. Once you
understand the language of each description, what is there
to be described in each is a matter of fact.[15]

Reformers or rationalizers?   Let me state at this point that I
am not without sympathy for the Perspectivalist approach to

"preserving the person." That it is a definite improvement over the reductionism of Evans's Capitulators would seem self-evident. It is clear that the Perspectivalist is appropriately and refreshingly modest regarding the explanatory potential of the natural-science approach, holding that it cannot deliver an exhaustive or metaphysically ultimate picture of the complexities of human action and interaction. Consequently the Perspectivalist is more than willing to grant the necessity of other approaches to human reality, such as the literary, the artistic, the historical or the religious. To the extent that it does this, Perspectivalism has contributed to the relativization of science in general and to the demise of overbearing scientism in psychology particularly.

But a crucial qualifier must be made at this juncture. Despite his or her modesty regarding the limits of natural science, the Perspectivalist still adheres strongly to what Evans calls the *unity of science thesis*. This thesis states that there is only one method which all genuine sciences employ, and that such a method consists of giving deterministic, causal explanations which are empirically testable.[16] In other words, the Perspectivalist will tolerate no tampering with the traditional definition or supposed purity of the natural-science approach, even though he or she concedes that this approach can yield only partial truth about whatever it studies. Thus the Perspectivalist who is a psychologist holds that this discipline must continue to use a natural-science methodology and no other, relegating to other fields (such as the humanities) the search for other perspectives on human functioning.

My point till now has been to demonstrate not merely that the natural-science approach to human psychological functioning has limited explanatory potential (although I trust I have done at least that), but that it is not the neutral, purely rational tool that Perspectivalists seem to believe it to be. It is, as Kuhn and others continue to show, a much more subjective and value-laden undertaking than most natural scientists admit.[17]

In addition, I have tried to show that, when applied to any but the simplest human functions, the natural-science approach is self-defeating because it insists on ignoring or trying to circumvent the *reflexive* character of human actions—that is, the capacity of persons to transcend and change the limitations of their circumstances merely by knowing about them and reflecting on them.

Interestingly, MacKay is very aware of this reflexive capacity of human beings; indeed, he takes it as one logical demonstration of the existence of human freedom.[18] But he does not take it (as I do) to be an indication that the natural-science approach in psychology should be either replaced or augmented by a different approach. Rather, he takes the position of most North American psychologists that however hard it may be to observe people in detail without thereby stimulating them to an involved reflexivity, it is the duty of all social scientists continually to strive for this methodological ideal.[19]

There are other problems with the Perspectivalists' resolution of the personalist/mechanist dilemma. One is the challenge of "relating what has been sundered"[20] or, in other words, showing how these various, equally important perspectives on persons fit together. If my behavior (for example, in writing this book) can be regarded both as the inevitable result of natural and historical causes and as a meaningful and rational personal choice, how are these two accounts to be related, especially when they seem so contradictory? Furthermore, how are we to keep the latter account from being reduced to the former, especially when the mechanistic view seems to be both more parsimonious and more immediately useful in terms of its capacity for prediction and control of events in the real world? In other words, how is the Perspectivalist to avoid becoming what one of my students labeled "a closet Capitulator"—that is, someone who pays lip service to the need for a variety of theoretical perspectives on the person, yet in fact supports and practices only the mechanistic account?

This is, in fact, what appears to be the present case in psychology at large. It is fair to say that nowadays almost all North American psychologists are token Perspectivalists, at least to the degree that they no longer claim a natural-science account of persons to be the ultimate one. Indeed, many recently written introductory texts concede right at the beginning that psychological topics can be approached from a variety of viewpoints. But such concessions amount to mere lip service simply because they are still not accompanied by any substantial changes in the conduct of the discipline itself: after the first-chapter qualifiers, even the most recent texts are largely devoted to an elaboration of natural-scientific research in psychology.

In addition, training procedures, research funding policies and judgments of scholarly competence continue to be made largely according to natural-scientific criteria. And at the institutional level, there is no evidence that departments of psychology are ready to share their still relatively great affluence with humanities departments in danger of closing down for lack of enrollments; incoming students, still naively expecting psychology to supply final answers about the puzzles of personhood, are not normally urged by psychology advisers to take as many or more courses in literature, history, philosophy or religion in order to balance the picture. On the contrary, these other perspectives, although agreed to be so essential, continue to languish further, while the high enrollments in psychology and other positivistically oriented social sciences continue relatively unabated. Such a situation bespeaks, at best, a culture lag between the desire for reform and the development of means for its implementation and, at worst, a calculated opportunism which continues to reap the benefits of public support for an approach even after its power is known to be vastly overrated.

Perspectivalism, then, is neither unique to Christians nor, in itself, an adequate means of "preserving the person." Both on the theoretical and the practical level, it all too easily slips back to the mechanistic determinism of Evans's Capitulators. In addition, even if this type of slippage is overcome, there still remains the problem of "putting Humpty Dumpty back together again." In other words, even where psychological, literary, historical, biological and other perspectives on the person are equally valued, supported and developed, the end result is still a fragmented human being rather than one who acts and reacts, thinks and feels, works and plays all of one piece. At a time when theologians and biblical scholars are rediscovering Scripture's emphasis on the entire, undivided person as the image of God and the responder to his initiatives,[21] it seems especially surprising that Christian psychologists remain content with a compartmentalized, multiperspectivalized approach to their object of study.

Yet Evans's research makes it clear that Perspectivalism has many adherents among evangelical scholars in the natural and social sciences. Given both the weaknesses of this approach and its continued support by so many in the evangelical community, it seems pertinent to consider why it remains such an attractive way of resolving the personalist/mechanist dilemma. I will consider two possible historical reasons for its staying power, one hearkening back to the last century, the other to the decades immediately preceding our own.

Perspectivalism considered historically. In his recent landmark work, *Fundamentalism and American Culture*, historian George Marsden points out that the dispensationalist thinking which dominated much of conservative Christianity around the turn of the century "was characterized by a dual emphasis on the supernatural and the scientific."[22] Like today's Christian Perspectivalists, the leaders of the dispensationalist movement believed both that the methods of natural science were objective and reliable, and that they could be employed to discover truth in all areas to which they were applied—and that, to the dispensationalists, included the Bible.

This concern of dispensationalists to be scientific never went so far as to embrace the sophistications of the experimental method. Dispensationalists did, however, emphasize reasoning from particular observations to general conclusions, after the manner laid down by seventeenth-century British scientist Francis Bacon and revived in the nineteenth-century Scottish philosophical movement known as Common Sense Realism.[23] When applied to the analysis of Scripture, says Marsden, this meant that the Bible, although supernatural in origin, "was regarded as a compendium of facts [which] they needed only to classify ... and follow wherever they might lead." These biblical facts were held by dispensationalists to be absolutely reliable and precise—hence the conviction that one could literally calculate the number of years in the various dispensations or even anticipate scientific discoveries in the poetic language of the book of Job! In essence,

the disposition to divide and classify everything is one of the most striking and characteristic traits of dispensationalism. ... Dispensationalist leaders regarded these methods as the only scientific ones. Scofield, for example, contrasted his work to previous "unscientific" systems. Reuben Torrey depicted his work as "simply an attempt at a careful unbiased, systematic, thorough-going inductive study and statement of Bible truth.... The methods of modern science are applied to Bible study: thorough analysis followed by careful synthesis."[24]

This does not mean that evangelical leaders were not also able to approve of the more experiential and pietistic elements of nineteenth-century Christianity. We all know that they were. As Marsden puts it, "Evangelical professors who insisted on not going beyond the careful arrangement of the facts could, at the same time, champion the popular romanticism and 'religion of the heart' of the revivals."[25] The rational and the experiential aspects of faith were thus both accorded a place.

There is something strangely schizophrenic, yet familiar, about this seesawing back and forth between an extreme biblical scientism on the one hand and an experiential and emotional religion of the heart on the other. Indeed, it looks rather like the Perspectivalism which is so current among evangelical social scientists today: on the one hand, a scientific apprehension of truth; on the other hand, a nonscientific one—both said to be essential, yet somehow never really unified.

I am suggesting that there may be a fairly direct relationship between one's approach to the handling of Scripture and one's approach to the doing of psychology—or indeed any of the other natural or social sciences. If a Christian student of psychology is heir to a tradition which gives "the methods of modern [i.e., natural] science" unquestioned pride of place in the interpretation of Scripture, it should not be surprising that those methods begin to take on the sacred quality of Scripture. This is not to suggest that today's Christian Perspectivalists are necessarily all naive chartmakers of the sort who painstakingly parallel Daniel's "sealed book" with the "seven-sealed book" of Revelation to discover the keys to world history, both past and future.[26] But a residual tendency remains among evangelical scientists to view the truth criteria of Scripture rather narrowly in terms of what can be proven to be positively true in the historical and natural-scientific senses of the word only. That scriptural truth may come packaged in many other forms, needing other methodologies to do it justice, seems to be only vaguely conceded and hardly developed as to its implications.[27]

Clearly, when I speak of such issues I am trespassing on sensitive and controversial ground. It is neither my place nor my purpose to make pronouncements on the current debate about scriptural inerrancy, even though I believe that its ultimate resolution can have significant implications for the doing of psychology by Christians. At this point, I am merely trying to outline what seems to be a major historical force behind the continuing preference of evangelical social scientists for the Perspectivalist position with its strong insistence that science must be unified around a natural-science ideal.

I am not alone, however, in suggesting a relationship between one's biblical hermeneutic and the approach to one's profession. For instance, economist Kenneth Elzinga has attempted a preliminary typology of five different ways in which Christian economists try to integrate their faith with their discipline, in both its theoretical and its applied aspects. Elzinga concludes that liberal and conservative economists who are also Christians will tend to invoke different parts of Scripture to support their respective liberal or conservative economic analyses. "The problem in formulating a Christian view of economic order," Elzinga says, "is not so much the ideology we bring to our *economics*, but rather the ideology we bring to our *hermeneutics*."[28]

In another significant area, that of political decision making in Washington, a recent ground-breaking study has shown that even among members of Congress who are classically theistic and affirm the divinity of Christ, at least four different hermeneutics (or what the authors of the study called "religious belief packages") are distinguishable and can be related to voting patterns which run the gamut from extreme conservatism to extreme liberalism. To come even close to predicting a given evangelical congressman's vote on an issue, the authors conclude, "you need to know how he interprets his religion, not merely how he labels it."[29]

In all of this, of course, the knotty question remains: does one's hermeneutic determine one's disciplinary approach, or is the situation reversed, or are hermeneutic and disciplinary approach mutually influential? I have suggested that in the case of Christian Perspectivalism, a particular hermeneutic tradition in American evangelical history has helped to entrench the preference for a natural-science-based psychology, even while its adherents claim to be relativizing its power substantially. But there may be other reasons for the entrenchment among evangelical Christians of Perspectivalism, with its tenacious commitment to the natural-science approach. Is it possible, for instance, that Christians in psychology have participated unreflectively in the seduction of the social sciences by the keepers of power and wealth in our society? Have they been caught up in a vicious cycle which began when they were paid handsomely to produce hard results but were thereby committed to claim more for their approach than it could reasonably deliver?

The erudite sociologist Robert Nisbet, although committed in principle and practice to many traditional modes of social-scientific research, publicly condemned his fellow social scientists in the 1970s for "the special kind of *hubris* that attacked [them] during the 1950's. With only the slenderest resources, they not only accepted invitations from all the men of power in Washington and elsewhere, but actually started knocking on doors demanding invitations." Nisbet then went on to cite "the vastly *greater* affinity that built up throughout the 1950's and 1960's between the sciences generally [including the social sciences] and the military establishment," a union social scientists constantly justified by thin appeals to the "pure," "basic" or "theoretical" nature of their contract work. The ultimate result of all this, wrote Nisbet, was the emergence of an entrenched entrepreneurship among the physical and social sciences "through which research started to be marketed by the piece and by the hour" to the highest bidder.[30]

Among psychologists, the forces cited by Nisbet have contributed to a species of vulgar pragmatism which has not gone unnoticed by thoughtful members of the profession. Several have pointed out that most graduate programs provide almost no training in theory construction: the emphasis is on devising efficient techniques to test ideas, not on generating provocative ideas to test by a methodology appropriate to the question.[31] Indeed, one respected social psychologist has concluded that "social psychologists have done no more than to operationalize questions and answers which were imagined elsewhere" and to characterize such an endeavor "not as the work of scientific analysis, but that of engineering."[32]

Clearly, I cannot document the extent of Christians' actual participation in this social-scientific entrepreneurship of the past three decades. But at the very least they have not protested it, and many seem to have been more than a little impressed by it. However misguided it may be, it has been one of the forces contributing to the persistence of an unreflective positivism in psychology. To put it bluntly, it is easy to convince oneself that a given mode of investigation is above reproach as long as it is being handsomely financed. But in an era of economic recession, psychologists may be more inclined to pay attention to the anomalies which have been within the discipline all along and to consider more seriously the possibility of fundamental reform. Moreover, the present state of both economic and paradigmatic uncertainty in psychology presents Christians with an opportunity to shape such reform instead of simply waiting to see what the world of secular scholarship will decide. What direction, then, might such reforms take?

Beyond Perspectivalism. I have tried to argue the need for an approach to the study of persons richer than a Perspectivalism which insists on maintaining the traditional definition of science with its stress on cause-and-effect relations, probabilistic generalizations and an exaggerated separation of observer from human subject. Such an approach is at best limited and at worst guilty of claiming far more than it can deliver, both in terms of its own standards and in terms of its potential for understanding human beings. Nor can I opt for the Perspectivalist's implied solution of dividing the labor—that is, letting the social sciences preserve the purity of the natural-science approach, however flawed it may be, and assigning to the arts and the humanities the study of the unique, the purposive and the integrated aspects of persons.[33]

I would insist, rather, that the traditional natural-science approach of psychology must be at least augmented, if not replaced, by a very different approach, based not on the continuity of human beings with lower organic and inorganic forms but on their unique differences from them. What research traditions already exist to facilitate such changes? Where have they led psychologists who have followed them? And what benefits, as well as hazards, may Christians expect in the pursuit of such alternatives? We will consider such questions before leaving the Sorcerer's Apprentice to continue his journey into the future.

Humanizers of Science

Evans delineates three broad ways psychologists have attempted to "preserve the person" in the face of the dominant, mechanistic paradigm. So far, however, we have dealt with only two of his three categories: the Reinterpreters of the Person (among whom Evans includes Capitulators and Compatibilists) and the Limiters of Science (who subdivide into Territorialists and Perspectivalists). Evans's third category, to which we now turn, is what he calls the *Humanizers of Science*. Like the other two categories, this one subdivides into two types, which Evans calls *Particularists* and *Generalists*. The former are persons who do not quarrel with the natural-science approach when applied to subhuman phenomena, but who insist (as I do) that the unique nature of human beings requires a different approach to do it full justice. Evans's Generalists are even more radical and suggest (as Kuhn has) that it is naive to believe that even the physical and biological sciences really operate according to a textbook definition of science. In fact, they question whether a single natural-science approach exists, even for the traditional nonhuman sciences such as physics, chemistry and biology. For our purposes, however, it is sufficient to consider these two subtypes together inasmuch as both would insist, at the very least, on the necessity for paradigmatic reform in the social sciences of which psychology is a part.

It is significant that although the Humanizers of Science include many well-known and articulate partisans throughout the social sciences, Evans is unable to cite a single Christian working in this tradition. Who, then, are the social scientists who have argued in an academically rigorous way for a humanized approach to their disciplines? Two have already been mentioned in chapter one, the nineteenth-century German philosopher and historian Wilhelm Dilthey and his disciple Eduard Spranger. Other prominent names include Max Weber, the pioneer German sociologist, and British scholars R. G. Collingwood and Peter Winch.[34] Within psychology, "new paradigm" researchers argue in a variety of ways for approaches which transcend the problems of positivism.[35] The entire third-force humanistic movement stands in opposition to both the psychoanalytic and the behaviorist forces in psychology; its pioneers include psychologists Gordon Allport, Carl Rogers and Abraham Maslow.[36] And related to third-force psychology in some ways are the existential and phenomenological traditions which are slowly gaining momentum on this side of the Atlantic after a much longer incubation period in Europe.[37]

Needed: a new paradigm. I do not intend to give detailed accounts of each of these attempts to humanize psychology and the other social sciences—a task which would require a volume or more of its own. Nor am I going to argue for any single one of them as the specific paradigm of choice in psychology. Rather I will focus for the moment on three features, common to all of them, which I believe Christians must take seriously, not only in light of problems with the more traditional approaches but also in view of some biblical considerations regarding the nature of persons. These include (1) an emphasis on the significance of *reflexivity* in both investigators and the persons they study, (2) a concern for the uncovering of *meaning* in human activity, and (3) an emphasis on the *unity* of personal experience. Let us deal with these three features in order.

In chapter two we defined human reflexivity as the ability of persons in experiments at least partially to transcend experimental manipulations simply by thinking about them. We also mentioned, as a second example of reflexivity, the effect of the researcher's own reflections and expectations on the experimental situation. These processes are called *reactivity* in the case of subjects and *experimenter expectancy* in the case of investigators. Both these types of reflexivity are regarded within the traditional paradigm as methodological vexations to be overcome. By contrast, reformers in the human-science traditions insist that they are human characteristics of such significance that they should be central to one's entire research approach.

This means that rather than being distracted from or underinformed about the true purposes of the research, participants are told about it in careful detail and regarded as collaborators in the entire enterprise. It also means that, rather than trying to neutralize their own theoretical biases, immediate expectations and even "metaphysical commitments" (as Kuhn called them), researchers are urged to spell them out carefully before conducting their research and allow them to inform the conduct of their research and its subsequent write-up. Notice that while such changes do overcome many of the knotty ethical problems associated with the traditional approach, their primary justification is not moral but ontological: it is based on the premise that the reflexive capacity of both researchers and participants is so radically human and so basic to the research process and outcome that it makes more sense to work with it than to keep struggling to make it disappear.

The second conviction shared by human-science reformers is that human actions cannot be approached with the kind of empirical detachment the natural scientist uses when studying nonhuman events. A moving person is not in the same class as a moving object or even a moving animal. Indeed, two persons moving in exactly the same sense-perceivable fashion are probably not even reducible to each other. In other words, human actions cannot be adequately understood or explained by an appeal to the abstract, empirical laws that are the stuff of natural science. According to the Humanizers of Science, we understand a human action only when we understand that person's own ideas about the situation—in other words, only when we understand the situation's meaning for that person. By this standard a human-science approach (as opposed to a natural-science approach) requires the investigator to understand his or her subject empathically, to "get inside the mind" of the agent, to walk in his or her shoes. German philosophers, such as Dilthey, called this process of knowing the other from the inside Verstehen, which can be roughly translated as "empathic understanding."

Although such an approach has rarely been considered, let alone developed, in mainstream North American academic psychology, it has had no little influence in the fields of history, anthropology and sociology. According to Collingwood, the historian should be less concerned to reconstruct the causes of a past human action than to clarify its purpose or meaning. Similarly, the anthropological tradition in Britain and North America has stressed the necessity of understanding another culture from the inside or on its own terms as much as possible. And in sociology the participant-observer approach was made famous by Erving Goffman's celebrated look at mental asylums from his own position as a quasi-inmate.[38]

In all three disciplines, adherence to such a human-science approach is almost always accompanied by the use of a descriptive, qualitative methodology involving active dialog between the researcher and those researched, rather than a quantitative approach aiming at causal explanation which maximizes the detachment of investigators from their subjects. Although this human-science approach has been ignored in mainstream academic psychology, it is not underdeveloped in psychology as a whole. Indeed, it is probably safe to say that in counseling psychology the method of Verstehen, although called by other terms (such as "client-centered counseling"), is fast becoming the preferred and most widely taught approach.[39] Furthermore, in the fast-growing new area of cross-cultural psychology, one of the pivotal debates continues to be whether, in going into another culture, psychologists should bring the theories, methods and instruments of their home cultures; or whether they should, in effect, begin the psychological enterprise anew, starting from the history, world view, lifestyle and concerns of the group to be researched.[40]

A final characteristic which appears to unite human-science advocates is a concern for the *wholeness* of human experience. In contrast to the natural-science tendency to reduce, compartmentalize or abstract the experience of persons studied, a human-science approach seems concerned to preserve the textured, integrated pattern of the individual or group being studied. As one methodologist, Paul Diesing, expresses it:

> [This] standpoint includes the belief that human systems [and phenomena] tend to develop a characteristic wholeness or integrity. They are not simply a loose collection of traits or wants or reflexes or variables of any sort; they have a unity that manifests itself in nearly every part. Their unity may be that of a basic spirit or set of values that expresses itself throughout the system, or it may be that of a basic mode of production and distribution that more or less conditions everything else, or perhaps that of a basic personality that shapes all [else] to its own needs and drives. Or the unity may not have any focal point, but may consist merely of myriad interweavings of themes and subsystems in a complex pattern. [Holistic researchers may] disagree on whether this organic unity of human systems . . . derives from some basic source—religion, ethics, technology, personality—but they agree that the unity is there.[41]

Implications of a humanized psychology.   There exist already, then, human-science traditions which recognize the importance of *reflexivity, meaning* and *wholeness* in human experience and activity. If these traditions are pointing to matters of unavoidable significance in human functioning, then they have implications for the way Christian psychologists should view their discipline and, inevitably, for the way that the discipline must view its own future.

Why, in the first place, are these human-science concerns

for reflexivity, meaning and wholeness important for Christians to note? It is not merely that, as God's servants in the world, we have a duty to keep abreast of the controversies which come and go in our various disciplines or professions. The biblical drama itself is shot through with the *fundamental givenness* of reflexivity, meaning and wholeness in human experience and activity; therefore we must approach those aspects of our discipline which ignore or try to circumvent these features with a biblically critical and reforming frame of mind.

At this point we will only hint at the biblical case for these three aspects of human experience. With regard to *reflexivity*, we can see that the writer of Ecclesiastes assumes that his readers are capable of attaining heightened self- and social awareness and also of revising their way of life based on this awareness. Indeed, the very nature of Scripture as a whole (not to mention the efforts made throughout history to preserve and disseminate it) assumes that its readers are not only capable of understanding its message, but also of acting (or choosing not to act) on the implications of that message.

With regard to the importance of *meaning*, we need to go no further than the Decalogue and the Sermon on the Mount, both of which refer not only to actions themselves (e.g., adultery, murder, theft), but also to the importance of the meaning behind the actions (e.g., lust, hate, covetousness). Indeed, the biblical distinction between homocide and murder which runs through Western jurisprudence to this day shows that the meaning of an act can make the difference between life and death. (It is significant, but not surprising, that many social scientists working in the positivist tradition take the position that such distinctions between action and intention should be abolished as reflective of an outmoded religious theory of human nature and accountability—a position that C. S. Lewis vehemently countered in both his *Abolition of Man* and his paper "The Humanitarian Theory of Punishment.")[42]

Finally, with regard to the importance of *wholeness* (in the sense of both interconnectedness and unifying theme), G. C. Berkouwer summarizes the current state of biblical scholarship when he says:

> We can say that in our times, under the influence of Biblical research, a fairly general consensus of opinion has arisen among theologians. They are increasingly conscious of the fact that the Biblical view of man shows him to us in an impressive diversity, but that it never loses sight of the unity of the whole man, but rather brings it out and accentuates it. No part of man is emphasized as independent of other parts, because the Word of God is concerned precisely with the whole man in his relation to God.[43]

It is true that Berkouwer goes on to say that the various terms and concepts used about human beings in the Bible give us "no exactly expressed or scientifically useful definitions," and that many Christian psychologists have taken this as a mandate for a perspectivalist approach. (When they want to refer to the whole person, they will appeal to religion and theology; when they want to develop an understanding of the detailed, separate human functions, they will appeal to the natural, social and behavioral sciences.) But my point is just the opposite: it is precisely because of Scripture's emphasis on the integrity and responsiveness of the whole person that we should insist on a psychology which does not systematically neglect the wholeness of persons in either their integrated patterning of experience and behavior or in the ground motives from which such patterning may take its cue.

But giving greater significance to reflexivity, meaning and wholeness is a concern not only of Christian psychologists. The challenge of a new human-science paradigm, were it to become substantial, would affect the entire conduct of mainstream psychology. First, the reflexive activity of both researchers and their subjects would cease to be treated merely as methodological embarrassments, and ways would be found to work with it rather than against it. This is a task which human-science reformers have themselves barely begun; indeed, they appear still to be at the stage of clarifying the various uses of the term *reflexivity* and understanding the ways in which reflexive persons change not only themselves but each other and the research process.[44] But it is at least clear that human-science research attempts already differ from the positivistic tradition in being more descriptive, qualitative and cooperative.

Second, uncovering meaning in the individual or group experience being studied would begin to replace casual explanation as an adequate goal of research. Given the historic American preoccupation with predictability, control and practical application in psychology, this would represent a significant shift of priorities. A concern for meaning would, in addition, undermine the still entrenched tendency to emphasize the relationship between overt behavior and identifiable environmental events to the relative neglect of cognitive and phenomenological processes. And yet, paradoxically, the task of uncovering meaning is not without practical significance itself—at least if we are to believe theorists like Viktor Frankl, whose basic therapeutic premise is that the psychological health of individuals (and, by extension, groups and even nations) depends on the degree to which they are able to discover the pattern of meaning—one might almost say the organizing myths—of their experience.[45]

Finally, a human-science revolution in psychology would probably not occur without a significant shift in the superordinate loyalties of psychologists from powerful institutions to the less powerful individuals and groups which make up the bulk of humankind everywhere. Until now, psychologists have primarily sought funding from (and hence tended to reflect the concerns of) large, monied societal institutions, in particular the granting agencies connected with government, business and industry. All of these institutions (as I have suggested in chapter two) find the atomistic, probability-centered findings of psychological research potentially useful in predicting sales, votes or the economic feasibility of government programs. But it is in these same fragmented, probabilistic generalizations that the unique and integrated aspects of persons, groups and phenomena are lost, and it is precisely such patterns that a humanized social science is concerned to recover. Such a shift of loyalties might well mean that psychologists would have less research money and fewer consulting jobs—but, on the other hand, it would also herald a period of greater independence and a chance for the discipline to let its subject matter, rather than the priorities of powerful institutions, shape its approach.

Psychologists would have to be prepared to tolerate a lot of ambiguity as they shift from a paradigm which has tended to ignore reflexivity, meaning and wholeness to the development of one which accords these features a central place. For many people, this would not be easy; academic life is always much more routine and predictable in periods of normal science. But although all three of these reforms would entail certain adjustments on the part of the psychological establishment, they would also bring some not insignificant benefits.

The chief of these, I suggest, would be a substantial reduction in the schizophrenia that exists in the lives of most academic psychologists and, indeed, in the discipline as a whole. We considered in chapter two the problems and contradictions that result when a morally conscientious psychologist attempts to generate a professional code of ethics in the face of an overwhelmingly amoral, deterministic disciplinary paradigm, or when psychologists whose entire scholarly lives presuppose their own reflexivity spend their lives studying other persons as if they were nonreflexive, mechanistically determined entities of the sort studied by the physical and biological sciences.[46] I have suggested that a substantial price has been exacted by such contradictions, both in terms of disciplinary progress and the integrity of psychologists' own lives.

In addition, there is the prominent gulf that divides the ruling paradigm of *academic* psychology from that of the *clinical* and *counseling* side of the profession. Earlier in this chapter I mentioned that variations on the Verstehen approach are becoming preferred modes in counseling and clinical psychology. This has not always been the case; in the past there have been pressures on these areas of psychology to adopt a positivistic paradigm (for example, by looking to medical or behavioral models of diagnosis and therapy), and a tendency to regard counseling or clinical psychologists who did otherwise as second rate. With the advent of a human-science psychology, the direction of influence would be, if anything, reversed, with academic psychologists looking to the Verstehen traditions of their clinical-counseling colleagues for hints as to how they themselves might proceed.[47]

Some lingering misconceptions. By way of summary, I have suggested three main characteristics which seem to distinguish a human-science approach from a natural-science approach to the study of persons: a recognition of the fundamental importance of human reflexivity, an emphasis on the uncovering of meaning and a concern with the undivided wholeness of human experience. I have further suggested that the reform of mainstream psychology to include such emphases would have three significant implications: first, the eclipse of positivistic research methods by ones which are more descriptive, qualitative and cooperative; second, the setting aside of causal explanation as the ultimate criterion for judging the adequacy of an investigative endeavor; and finally, a shift of allegiance on the part of psychologists from the concerns of large and powerful institutions to those of ordinary people of every sort.

Clearly these reforms and their implications are interrelated; clearly too they will not be actualized quickly. Paradigm shifts do not occur overnight: for not only do they involve changes in theoretical focus (indeed, Kuhn would go further and say changes in one's entire view of the order of nature), but also changes in research methods and instruments, in training procedures, and in publication and funding policies. Moreover, to compound these difficulties, mainstream psychology labors under at least two fundamental misconceptions about the human-science approach. Each of these merits a brief mention.

The first misconception is that the human-science enterprise assumes each person's experience is so personal and subjective as to be unknowable by anyone else who attempts to investigate it. Clearly, if this were the case, any investigative attempt would be doomed from the outset, and the human-science paradigm with it. But it is just this solipsistic view of persons which the human scientist is at pains to deny. The life world *(Lebenswelt)* of the reflexive human agent is irreducibly *intersubjective* or *communal*. That is to say, it correctly assumes a basic like-mindedness in others and constantly acts upon this belief. If this were not the case, even the most ordinary human conversation would be as impossible as a conversation between a person and a dog! But in reality, we share not only a common, external world about which to converse but also a common capacity to experience each other's actions in terms of their rational bases as well as their motives, meanings and goals.

In fact, as Evans points out, "without this everyday awareness of the other as personal agent, even [traditional] science, which is a communal activity, would be impossible. That is, the [psychologist] who writes papers about human beings as stimulus-conditioned organisms still writes those papers for scientists whom he assumes are conscious, rational beings, able to perceive and understand the meaning of his words and deeds and to respond in rationally appropriate ways."[48] Human experience, then, is not merely subjective; it is also, to a very high degree, intersubjective. It is this very intersubjectivity that the human scientist wishes to take advantage of in wake of its long history of official neglect by mainstream social science. He further wishes to develop alternative research strategies which depend upon it.

It should be pointed out, however, that the mistaken view of human science as inevitably solipsistic has an understandable basis in recent North American history. Beginning in the mid-

1950s, the humanistic psychology movement in North America set out to protest and change the monopoly held by both behaviorist and psychoanalytic orientations in psychology. Unfortunately for both the movement itself and psychology at large, the much publicized development of humanistic psychology in the 1960s was in the direction of an ever increasing emphasis on isolated individual experience. This emphasis appeared to take two forms—first, an epistemological statement—individual experience is so unique that no other individual can adequately share it; second, an ethical statement—the individual's private experience is the primary (if not the only) criterion for making value judgments of any kind.

Mainstream psychology was concerned about humanistic psychology's adherence to both these types of individualism, but especially the first inasmuch as it seemed to undermine the bedrock assumption that science is concerned to investigate patterns which transcend individual differences. And indeed the traditional psychologists' fear of creeping solipsism seemed more than confirmed in the much repeated slogan of innumerable encounter group alumni: "I know you believe you understand what you think I said, but I'm not sure you realize that what you heard is not what I meant." We shall return to the distortions of ethical individualism in the final pages of this chapter, but at this point we mention the epistemological solipsism of humanistic psychology as one (but only one) reason for the psychological establishment's premature rejection of a human-science paradigm.

But if a human-science paradigm, rightly understood, begins with the assumption that persons can engage in mutual, understandable dialog about each other's experience, this hints at a second misconception about the paradigm which needs to be mentioned. If human beings share a capacity for mutual dialog, does this mean that the fruits of such dialog can always be taken at face value? This is a question posed both by academic psychologists in the positivist camp and by clinicians and counselors in the psychoanalytic tradition, for both these traditions seem committed to profound skepticism on this very point. That is to say, both (although in somewhat different ways) maintain from the outset that persons studied by psychologists cannot be trusted to give an accurate, unbiased account of their own experience and behavior. The psychoanalytic tradition assumes that the person (whether deeply neurotic or only mildly so) has an intricate network of unconscious defense mechanisms—such as repression, denial, projection and regression—which protect the ego from facing unpleasant truths about the self. Only the expert analyst (part of whose training has involved his or her own extended psychoanalysis at the hands of another expert) is capable of seeing what is really going on in the patient, and then only with difficulty can the expert lead him or her to the same insights.

Positivistic psychology assumes, first of all, that persons are so intimately bound up with their own experience that they cannot possibly report it with any consistent accuracy. Indeed, it is difficult even for the expert to observe what is really happening to another without the help of methodological tricks to reduce the effects of observer bias—but at least this latter strategy is infinitely more capable of objectivity than is reliance on first-person reports. Furthermore, because positivistic psychology is committed to explaining human behavior in terms of impersonal forces of nature and nurture, it constantly attempts to demonstrate ways in which people are in fact at the mercy of impersonal forces when they believe that their behavior is under their own control. This debunking function is part of the object of doing experiments—especially in social and personality psychology.

Thus the interpretive principle, or hermeneutic, of both psychoanalytic and positivistic psychology (unlike that of a human-science psychology) is, in Paul Ricoeur's words, "not an explication of the object, but a tearing off of masks, an interpretation that reduces disguises.... [It] looks upon the whole of consciousness as 'false' consciousness."[49] What is the human scientist's response to such skepticism about his or her own assumptions regarding the trustworthiness of both participants in the dialogal process?

Perhaps the most radical opposition to it comes from the phenomenological camp descended from Edmund Husserl which takes the individual human being as the center of a system of coordinates on which the experience of the world is mapped, and insists that human experience is the major, trustworthy source of data about that world.[50] The inspection of this experience (whether in oneself or another) takes place by Husserl's method of phenomenological *reduction*, whereby the very influences held to be determinative by positivistic psychologists (individual background, cultural and intellectual assumptions) are systematically laid aside in order to look at the pure, unvarnished structures of conscious experience. Phenomenologists in this tradition also insist on the intersubjective verifiability of such an exercise and conclude that "the goal of phenomenology is to *describe the universal* structures of *subjective* orientation in the world, not [as in positivistic social science] to explain the *general* features of the *objective* world."[51]

Is such pure, rational apprehension of one's own (or anyone else's) experience possible? Thinkers in the post-Kuhnian tradition would certainly say no, for if prescientific ideas about the order of nature invade our study of the subhuman world (as Kuhn demonstrated), how much more will they affect our study of other human beings? In other words, just as the physicist, chemist or biologist is shaped by the discipline's ruling paradigm to see selectively—that is, to see things more easily in terms of the accepted paradigm than in any other terms—so will psychologists inevitably see their subject matter in terms of their own largely unarticulated ideas about the order of nature, whether these are shaped by a scientific paradigm, by extra-scientific beliefs, or by both.

Indeed, a phenomenological tradition somewhat different

from Husserl's suggests that this tendency is part of the human condition generally—and since even the most sophisticated methodological tricks cannot eliminate it, it should be consciously acknowledged as a vital feature of the scholarly enterprise.[52] This does not mean, however, that we return to a skeptical despair of objectivity which we apply to scientist and nonscientist alike. Rather it means that even before beginning a piece of research, investigators must investigate themselves. That is, they must consider seriously, not just individually but in community, how their preconceived views of human nature, of science and of their research topic interact with the research process. The final research product is then acknowledged to be a contribution to the accumulated knowledge on the topic, but one which is also inevitably *contextual*—that is, qualified by historical, personal and disciplinary forces acting on investigators and their research participants alike.

Even given these qualifications, the human scientist insists that psychologists should at least be no more skeptical about the research participants' capacity for accurate self-reflection than they are about their own. Gordon Allport has asserted that while it makes obvious sense to question the testimony of persons who are very young, very disturbed or very defensive about a given issue, nevertheless "too often we fail to consult the richest of all sources of data—namely, the subject's own self-knowledge." To support his confidence in the human capacity for accurate self-reflection, he refers to a World War 2 study of psychiatrists' success in screening candidates for the armed services: "While they employed various [objective] tests, it is said that the best predictive question turned out to be, 'Do you feel that you are emotionally ready to enter military service?' The men themselves were often the best judges—although not, of course, infallible."[53]

Having spent some time examining the characteristics and implications of a human-science approach in psychology, perhaps we can profit by looking at an actual example. In chapter two we considered the logic and limitations of a representative psychology experiment in the positivistic tradition. While there are many studies in the human-science tradition which could be examined by way of contrast to the "Misery Loves Company" study, it seems reasonable to choose one which studies the same phenomenon as that experiment—namely, human affiliation. In this way we may be able to see what a human-science approach can elicit about its subject matter which the natural-science approach cannot.

A Human-Science Case Study: "On Being Close Friends"

It will be recalled that the "Misery Loves Company" study examined, in an isolated, temporary setting, one factor (the anticipation of physical pain) which influences people to seek out the company of others. In that experiment both the composition of the experimental groups and the pressure to affiliate were contrived by the experimenter. Indeed, none of the participants knew each other before the experiment, and it is doubtful if any relationships were extended beyond it. But in reality the most important affiliative relationships between human beings are ongoing, freely chosen ones which change their character across time and circumstance and thereby defy the manipulations of the traditional experiment. Long-term, close friendships between same-sex adults are one example of such an affiliative relationship. Yet attempts by psychologists to answer the question "Why and in what way is Person A a friend of Person B?" have rarely gotten beyond answers such as residential proximity and interpersonal similarity—factors which are operative only in the preliminary, acquaintanceship stage of the friendship, yet are erroneously offered as its entire explanation.

But once a friendship has started, the challenge remains of making it work, and this process of friendship growth and maintenance remains largely unstudied. Indeed, according to one critic, the reluctance to abandon an experimental strategy (with its random assignment of subjects to conditions and its single-session manipulations) has resulted not in a psychology of friendship but a psychology of strangers.[54] Nor have nonexperimental studies of the survey/self-report type been able to move much beyond this, for although they examine friendship beyond the initial acquaintance stage and isolate such qualitative components as reciprocity, compatibility and admiration, they still fail to capture the context in which these factors operate and their experienced meaning in the friendship process.

It was just such limitations that Elizabeth Lines wished to overcome in her research into the phenomenon of "being close friends."[55] In selecting same-sex friendship pairs for her study, Lines decided to focus on persons in their thirties, on the grounds that the experience of noncollege age groups has been neglected and that their experience of friendship would undoubtedly be somewhat different from that of young adults with fewer responsibilities and an unsettled career pattern. Equal numbers of male and female pairs were studied with no constraints of marital status, but the total number of ten pairs was substantially less than is usual in a more positivistic strategy, where the phenomena to be studied are reduced to efficiently administered, operationalized variables to which many subjects can be exposed in a short space of time. By contrast, Lines's approach was to look at the structure of a smaller number of friendships, but to examine them much more exhaustively. Problems of representativeness still remain, but they are no worse than those that result from using the more traditional methodology. Lines's approach has the advantage of not reducing the studied phenomenon to constrained, operational definitions.

Several other features distinguish Lines's methodology from more traditional studies of affiliation. In the first place, contact with each friendship pair lasted at least a full month. In the second place, each participant not only was fully informed beforehand of the purpose and plan of the study, but was also shown the final structural summary of his or her friendship experience (as well as the metastructure resulting from the study of all ten experiences), in order to give critical feedback as to its perceived accuracy. In the third place, while the key data-gathering technique consisted of a structured interview, certain features distinguished it from more traditional interview techniques: the questions were fewer in number and more open ended. Moreover, they were given to participants several days before the actual interview in order to allow each to reflect on them at length and at leisure. Finally, no time limits were placed on the interview itself. Participants decided for themselves how much to say in response to each question or even whether to modify or go beyond them in the information provided. Similarly, the interviewer was free to make occasional probes for further clarification or explanation of the participants' comments. Such a process is termed a *dialogal interview*.

Here are the actual questions considered by the members of each friendship dyad:

1. Try to recall in detail your most recent experience with your friend.

2. Can you describe in what ways this is a close friendship? That is, can you think about the ways in which this friendship is different from others? What is it that makes this a close friendship?

3. Has there ever been a time when you felt your friendship was threatened? Was there ever a situation where you had to decide whether your friendship would end or continue—a crisis situation?

4. Have you ever had the experience of feeling far away—or distant—from your friend? Explain.

5. Can you describe a specific experience that you feel confirmed your friendship?

6. Many people feel that the ability and opportunity to speak intimately of yourself to another is a central feature of friendship. Do you think so? Could you give an example of this experience in your own friendship?

7. Have there been times in your relationship where problems or tensions have resulted from either "telling" or "not
telling" certain information?

These questions aimed at providing a setting—neither too con-
stricting nor too vague—in which the central features of close
friendship might emerge. The first question functioned essentially to encourage participants from the very start of the interview to focus on concrete experiences rather than abstract de-
scriptions. Other questions considered how the person knew
the relationship was a close one (questions 2 and 5), the maintenance aspects of the relationship (questions 3 and 4), and the
process by which the knowing and maintaining of the friendship occurred (questions 6 and 7).

Analyzing the ten transcribed interviews involved identify-
ing significant statements in which the speakers referred directly to friendship. The thematic meaning of each statement was
explicated, and similar themes were clustered according to their
shared or complementary nature. These clusters of themes were
then showed to the original participants for confirmation or
adjustment. At this point the researcher was essentially asking
each participant, "Do you recognize your friendship in these
clusters of themes? If there is some distortion in my thematizing
or clustering, show me where it is." With the (possibly revised)
theme clusters in hand, Lines then attempted to arrive at an exhaustive description of the topic—that is, one which catches
the essence of all the clusters of themes.

In this study, approximately thirty significant statements
were explicated; they included themes such as "willingness to
go out on a limb for the other," "total acceptance without conditions or qualifications," "a lot of talking," "sharing private
information," "knowing when to keep your mouth shut," and
"threat of perceived changes in each other." In the process of
clustering these themes, Lines and her respondents agreed that
it was almost as if friendship were the third member in what
exists objectively as a two-person relationship—an independent

structure created by the self-other dyad. The clusters of themes refer to this "third life" and how it shows itself.

More specifically, the themes seem to cluster around friendship as possessing (1) *comfort* ("it is a home and refuge in which unqualified love pervades without competition or threat of punishment"; "it promotes pleasure in giving and sharing"; "it seeks to promote growth through supportiveness and protection"); (2) *power* ("it commands respect as a unique, invaluable creation of self and other, requiring priority treatment"; "it must contend with the world at large and ward off interference that threatens its stability"; "it allows a limited freedom, restraining radical change in order to preserve itself and maintain balance"); and (3) *transcendence* ("it combines self and other into a sensing, feeling whole"; "it creates a life larger than that of each individual, in a sense completing the individual"; "it outlasts the constraints of any given point in its history").

Let me emphasize that I have not reported this study in order to recommend its methodology as the ideal or only one for a psychology reformed along human-science lines; the interested reader can pursue both it and others by referring to the appropriate (and rapidly expanding) list of resources.[56] But Lines's method has features in common with others in the developing human-science tradition which we may summarize by contrasting with some of the problems of the positivistic approach laid out in chapter two. In all human-science-influenced investigative methods, the reflexivity which the investigator takes for granted in himself or herself is both assumed and invoked in the study's participants. Far from being given incomplete or misleading information about the study, participants are fully informed as to its object and procedure, and their corrective view of the results is considered an essential step in the validation process. Phenomena are studied in their naturally occurring contexts without the problems of informed consent and legal accountability which plague traditional field experiments. And finally there is substantial evidence that studies in the human-science tradition are perceived as rewarding and beneficial by the participants themselves, whose attempts to explicate the nature and meaning of an important life phenomenon in the context of a relationship of collaboration and mutual respect with the investigator add to their own process of self-understanding.

But let me also emphasize that, in calling for self-conscious reform in psychology along human-science lines, I am not suggesting that the natural-science approach should thereby be outlawed. It is possible that, for all its limitations and ethical problems, there are situations in which it will remain the approach of choice. But I believe that we need to think out more clearly just what kinds of situations these might be. For because of its heavily forged link to technology, the natural-science approach is often deeply—if unconsciously—committed to ideals of efficiency and profit. In psychology, this has shown itself particularly in the tendency to make manipulations and measurements as condensed and swift as prediction of isolated bits of behavior in an acceptable percentage of people will allow. My suspicion is that this kind of practice should be restricted to emergency situations and not be considered normative.

For example, the use of early IQ tests for the imperfect sorting of soldiers into potential officers and other ranks in World War 1 may, with all its limitations, have been the only possible compromise, given the pressures of the times. But to turn such emergency procedures using captive populations into the normative model for psychological research on the complexities of contextualized, reflexive, accountable persons is rather like looking through the wrong end of the telescope forever.

The human-science reforms which we have discussed are, it seems to me, ones which Christians should welcome and encourage to a large degree. To the extent that they protest the traditional *hubris*, or exaggerated self-confidence of the natural-science tradition, to the extent that their attitude toward human research subjects stresses respect and collaboration rather than routine suspicion and objectification, to the extent that they elevate understanding and insight to a position of comparable respect with the goals of predictability and control, they are much needed reforms in the realization of which Christians ought to be vanguard participants, not reluctant stragglers. And yet we must make some final qualifications from a biblical perspective, and it is in light of these qualifications that we will not only send the Sorcerer's Apprentice on his way but also offer him a road map for the journey ahead.

Beyond Human Science: Some Critical Christian Comments

The reader who is somewhat familiar with the human-science landscape in psychology will have noticed that I have neither tried to give an exhaustive survey of specific human-science movements nor proclaimed a preference for one or another of them. Rather, I have concentrated on certain general features which I consider significant. This decision was motivated not only by the constraints of space but also by a conviction that no one of the developing movements provides an adequate paradigm, in itself, for a reformed psychology—even though all are competing for a place in the disciplinary sun. Indeed, when one surveys the writings of various humanistic, phenomenological, existential, dialectical, cognitive and transpersonal psychologists, it seems that beyond their common rejection of the positivist status quo and their common commitment to the importance of reflexivity, meaning and integration in the study of persons, these movements tend to see each other as rivals. In fact, one is sometimes reminded of competing national liberation movements, all concerned to topple the colonial overlord, but each equally determined that it will be the exclusive ruling party in the new regime.

This exclusivism, I would venture to say, is motivated by competing, underlying "control beliefs," or presuppositions about reality, that no amount of reflexive self-investigation or resentment of a common foe can completely transcend.[57] For as

Kuhn has pointed out, paradigms involve not only methodological and conceptual convictions, but metaphysical ones as well. Consequently, thoughtful Christian scholars need to isolate and qualify such assumptions in the human-science camp in light of their own biblically grounded convictions about the nature of reality and of human activity—including scientific activity. What I am suggesting is that the human-science enterprise is a two-edged sword: on the one hand, its proponents are persons created in the image of God who are consequently capable of discovering truths about the world and its inhabitants after the manner recorded by Paul in Romans 1. That they have corporately made a case for aspects of human functioning which must be foundational in any psychology of persons should by now be fairly clear. On the other hand, human-science proponents are as much products of humanity's Fall as anyone else, and just as prone to worship the creation rather than the Creator —albeit in different ways from their positivistic colleagues.

This means that we must be alert to distortions which, notwithstanding the admirable program of basic reforms we have discussed, threaten to lead psychology's various human-science movements into self-defeating contradictions just as paralyzing as those they have identified in the positivistic status quo. What are these distortions? I will mention those which seem to me to be the most salient, beginning with two that have been mentioned already in the section devoted to the implications of a humanized psychology.

First of all, there is the very real danger of a human-science psychology becoming an anarchistic cult of the individual self. Despite the care that its more scholarly proponents have taken to develop canons of intersubjective verifiability and to stress the irreducibly communal nature of human experience in general and scholarship in particular, it is very easy for persons to jump from a legitimate criticism of natural science's neglect of the individual to the opposite abuse of absolutizing individual autonomy and denying any communal norms and obligations (including those of corporate scholarship) which do not happen to suit one's own immediate tastes.

We have already seen such distorted control beliefs at work to the detriment of the humanistic psychology movement, and nowhere has their influence on society at large been more trenchantly documented and criticized than in personality theorist Paul Vitz's *Psychology as Religion: The Cult of Self-Worship.* In his analysis of a variety of self-theorists and their popularizers, Vitz traces a consistent belief—unquestioned and unverified—in the notion that the optimal development of the self comes from deliberately casting off all restrictions imposed or implied by others. At the same time, many of these same theorists assert that such selfishness does not, in fact, promote neglect of others; on the contrary, it is held that mistreatment of others is the by-product of failure to put one's own needs first, and conversely, that love of others will be the natural result of the total recovery of self-love and self-realization—a strange exercise in logic indeed!

Vitz suggests that humanistic self-psychology was able to engage in and promote such logical somersaults as long as naive confidence in unlimited economic expansion (so typical of America in the 1960s) allowed people to believe that there was room at the top for everyone. By contrast, Vitz remarks, "it has become very hard to actualize oneself at today's prices."[58] Thus the current shattering of assumptions about unlimited material progress is one factor which helps to unmask the naiveté of such hedonistic control beliefs. Indeed, it might be possible to argue that the human-science enterprise has developed in a more conscientious and scholarly way in Europe in part because, as the locus of two devastating world wars, Europe has been less prone to seduction by such an individualistic and economically overconfident philosophy. Nonetheless, the solipsism and narcissistic self-contemplation inherent in such assumptions remain no small threat to the development of a responsible human science—and it is precisely here that Christians, with their consciousness of human fallenness and their insistence on placing individual vocation within the context of communal responsibility, should strive to exercise a corrective influence.

Second, we have already alluded to the tendency of some human-science movements (in particular some forms of phenomenology) to assume a purity of human rationality that also cannot stand up to the test of experience. In assuming the possibility that all preconceptions, vested interests and ideologies can be set aside in order to allow a pure, descriptive analysis of one's own or another's consciousness, such traditions ignore not only the biblically implied consequences of the Fall on human thought and motivation, but also the considerable legacy left to us by Freud's lifetime work on the life of the unconscious. However doctrinaire and overgeneralized such psychoanalytic insights may themselves have been, their inherent skepticism is an essential corrective to a belief in the unlimited autonomy of human reason.

For psychologists, Christian and otherwise, the most practical challenge resulting from this tension between trusting and not trusting the fruits of reflection may be to decide when each is appropriate. As a preliminary rule of thumb, I would suggest that an attitude of trust can operate in most situations which are not experienced by their participants as primarily stressful or threatening—for it is in just such circumstances that defense mechanisms begin to operate. For example, it would probably have been unwise for Elizabeth Lines to include among her friendship dyads pairs of people whose friendships were on the brink of collapse or who suffered from grossly unequal commitments. Such stresses, while not eliminating the possibility of accurate self-description, do place considerable strains on it. Conversely, by seeking out mutually close friendships which had endured the test of time, she was more likely to optimize both the likelihood of accurate reflection and the likelihood that she would, in fact, be probing some essential features of being close friends.

Related to the above criticism is the danger that human science, in its stress on uniquely human capacities (such as reflexivity and the quest for meaning), may ignore the *creatureliness* of persons. For however much we may transcend the forces of nature and nurture which tyrannize lower organisms and lifeless phenomena, we can never leave them completely behind. We are not only related "upward" to the Creator of the universe, sharing his image and capacities, but also "downward" to the rest of his creation: from dust we come, to dust we will return. Consequently it may be inappropriate for Christians to suggest that a human-science psychology should totally eclipse the traditional natural-science approach. In some areas of psychology —notably those which study sensory processes and the physiological aspects of behavior—a mechanistic paradigm may still be the most appropriate in many instances, although even in these domains the operation of reflexivity may be considerable, as the burgeoning study of biofeedback continues to testify.

Nor would I totally reject the "debunking" quality of much traditional psychology—that is, its concern to show just how frequently we can be influenced to act against our better judgment by the forces of personal history, social influence or distorted perception. Although we should indeed resist the methods by which such influences are usually demonstrated and the overgeneralizations that result, it is not bad to know the fragility of our own sweet reasonableness. Such knowledge has been known to bring non-Christians to belief and Christians to a greater understanding of their dependence upon God as well as to a deeper appreciation of his grace in Jesus Christ.

If the admission of such a compromise makes me a Perspectivalist, it is Perspectivalism with a difference. For unlike the traditional Christian Perspectivalist I am insisting, at the very least, that a plurality of approaches, or perspectives, be *built right in* to the conduct of psychology, not merely acknowledged as a desirable norm across disciplines while still insisting on the hegemony of a natural-science approach in psychology. Moreover, such a Perspectivalism insists that the need for pluralism not merely be accorded lip service, but be accompanied by the necessary changes in the training, funding and evaluation standards of the discipline. And as an ultimate goal, it also aims at a new unity of science, one in which both the "upward" and "downward" aspects of persons—both their creatureliness and their *imago Dei*—can be considered together in their inevitable unity, not only in the persons studied by psychologists, but in the students and practitioners of psychology themselves.

Three final, interrelated dangers of the human-science revolution need to be mentioned. The first is that, in a concern to atone for the past excesses of detachment, superiority and manipulation in psychology, human-science reformers sometimes seem to be suggesting that all distinctions of rank should disappear and that psychologists can do no more than learn with— or even from—the people they once merely studied. While such an attitude is, in one sense, compatible with the biblical conviction that we are all ultimately of one rank before God, it is incompatible with the notion that gifts and offices do at times lead to distinctions of role and authority. Such a tension implies a responsibility on the part of a reformed psychology to avoid both the excesses of elitism and those of undifferentiated equality.

Related to this is a second tendency to see in the universality of human reflexivity a new kind of autonomous, superhuman potential. Sometimes such suggestions are even cloaked in a religious vocabulary (unthinkable to psychologists twenty years ago); at a recent, prestigious symposium on "The Future of Psychology" sponsored by the American Psychological Association, a participant said:

> Personally, I have been intrigued by the parallelism between changes in the scientific world view and those in theology. Do you remember the excitement about the "death of God" some years ago? The God who died then was an outsider God,

a God who bore to His creation a relation analogous to that of the 19th-century scientist to his object of study. He stood outside of His system, demonstrating His existence by occasional violation of His own laws to favor one or another of His human creatures. Newer theology tends to avoid the noun "God," but when human beings transcend the limitations of their deterministic past, they manifest what these new theologians see as divine. Faith becomes horizontal rather than vertical. Humanity co-creates itself, asserts this theology, in complete agreement with the newer science. Incidentally this newer theology is much easier to reconcile with Eastern religion than was the earlier version.[59]

It is precisely in relation to such statements that Christians must exercise discernment and counterinfluence, for although the vocabulary has theistic connotations, the sentiments are anything but biblical.

Finally, it should be pointed out that the human scientist's concern to uncover meaning in human experience may run the danger of seeing as significant only the process, and not the content, of such an exercise. In other words, in acknowledging the universality of the human quest for meaning, some deny the possibility that imputed meanings can be false or misleading; while others, such as Carl Rogers and Viktor Frankl, seem routinely to evade the question. Given the traditionally strident opposition of most psychologists to religion of any sort, it is easy for Christians to assume that any concession in psychology to the recovery of meaning and the irreducibility of the religious impulse is better than none. Even Vitz, in the last chapter of *Psychology as Religion,* praises the recent development in humanistic psychology of appreciation for and encouragement of mystical or "transpersonal" experience.[60] Yet not long ago I spoke with an old friend from my graduate student days who had just attended the annual convention of the Association for Humanistic Psychology. He confirmed to me that, in his words, "new and exciting spiritual emphases" were now largely replacing encounter groups as the most significant focus of the association's meetings. I was less than happy to find out that his own emergent spirituality had settled around a quasi-Hindu pantheism which no longer admitted of any ultimate distinction between good and evil.

Furthermore, it is not at all clear that persons having biblically based convictions and experiences, however meaningful or spiritual, would be welcome in many human-science circles, especially once they made clear their fundamental belief that Jesus Christ is "the way, and the truth, and the life" and not merely one of many paths to the same goal (the kind of spiritual pluralism which seems to be the emerging party line in psychology). Yet we must insist that it is not enough to get beyond a scientistic materialism to just any kind of deeper meaning or higher spiritual experience, however immediately positive. Rather we are urged as Christians not to "believe every spirit, but test the spirits to see whether they are of God; for many false prophets have gone out into the world" (1 Jn 4:1).

In a word, Christian exploration of the human-science landscape requires both discernment and strength of faith and character in the face of possible rejection. These qualifications must be part of our travel kit as we accompany the Sorcerer's Apprentice along his path into the future. Yet it may also be that his own unfamiliarity with the territory ahead will make him more, not less, open to counsel from those whose insights into the human condition are aided by revealed truth from the One who has created and offered redemption to all humankind. Having lost the former moorings of an idolatrous dependence on science, traditionally conceived, he may well, like Peter, come to ask, "Lord, to whom shall we turn?" Let us, for a change, not hang back to see what the world of secular scholarship will decide as the answer to such a question. Let us, rather, consider carefully how we can best share "the words of eternal life" and all their implications with the Sorcerer's Apprentice.

NOTES

Preface

[1]Sigmund Koch, "Psychology and Emerging Conceptions of Knowledge as Unitary," in *Behaviorism and Phenomenology: Contrasting Bases for Modern Psychology,* T. W. Wann ed. (Chicago: University of Chicago Press, 1964), pp. 4-5.

Chapter 1

[1]Robert Oppenheimer, "Analogy in Science," *American Psychologist* 11 (March 1956):127-35.

[2]See Hugh F. Kearney, *Science and Change, 1500-1700* (New York: McGraw-Hill, 1971), for one introduction to the development of science in Europe.

[3]*Encyclopaedia Britannica,* 15th ed., s.v. "History of Science," by Jerome R. Ravetz.

[4]See L. Kalsbeek, *Contours of a Christian Philosophy* (Toronto: Wedge Publishing Foundation, 1975), for a clear introduction to the structure, history and development of the concept of "sphere sovereignty."

[5]Aldous Huxley, *Ends and Means: An Inquiry into the Nature of Ideals and the Methods Employed for Their Realization* (London: Chatto and Windus, 1937).

[6]Bertrand Russell, *Why I Am Not a Christian* (London: Unwin Books, 1957), p. 113.

[7]For a thorough yet readable introduction to the history of psychology, both as a natural and a human science, see Henryk Misiak and Virginia S. Sexton, *History of Psychology: An Overview* (New York: Grune and Stratton, 1966). The classic volume on the history of American experimental psychology is Edwin G. Boring, *History of Experimental Psychology*, 2d ed. (Englewood Cliffs, N.J.: Prentice-Hall, 1950).

[8]A detailed treatment of the place of Protestant belief in the development of natural science can be found in Reijer Hooykaas, *Religion and the Rise of Modern Science* (Grand Rapids: Eerdmans, 1972).

[9]See Kalsbeek, *Contours*, chapters four and five; and (for a more basic treatment by a Christian philosopher) Herman Dooyeweerd, *A New Critique of Theoretical Thought*, vol. 1 (Philadelphia: Presbyterian and Reformed Publishing Company, 1953).

[10]For a more detailed treatment of the history of psychology as a human science, see Amedeo Giorgi, *Psychology as a Human Science: A Phenomenologically-Based Approach* (New York: Harper and Row, 1970), chapter one; and Misiak and Sexton, *History of Psychology*, chapters nine and ten.

[11]For an introduction to Dilthey's thinking, see Herbert A. Hodges, ed., *Wilhelm Dilthey: An Introduction* (London: Routledge, 1944).

[12]Quoted in Misiak and Sexton, *History of Psychology*, p. 354.

[13]Ibid., p. 137.

[14]Ibid., p. 128.

[15]Boring, *History of Experimental Psychology*, p. 518.

[16]Misiak and Sexton, *History of Psychology*, p. 138.

[17]Boring, *History of Experimental Psychology*, p. 527.

[18]Charles G. McClintock, Charles B. Spaulding and Henry A. Turner, "Political Orientations of Academically Affiliated Psychologists," *American Psychologist* 20, (March 1965):211-21.

[19]Paul C. Vitz, *Psychology as Religion: The Cult of Self-Worship* (Grand Rapids: Eerdmans, 1977), pp. 11-12. As the title implies, Vitz is mainly critiquing not the positivistic but the humanistic stream of North American psychology. However, he shares with me the conviction that much of the hostility to religion among psychologists is rooted in their own apostasy.

[20]Misiak and Sexton, *History of Psychology*, p. 145.

[21]Fred McKinney, "Fifty Years of Psychology," *American Psychologist* 31 (November 1976):834-42. McKinney makes a strong case for the conclusion that the major influence on the direction of American psychology has been the culture's demand for findings with applied value.

Chapter 2

[1]McClintock, Spaulding and Turner, "Political Orientations."

[2]Stanley Schacter, *The Psychology of Affiliation: Experimental Studies of the Sources of Gregariousness* (Stanford: Stanford University Press, 1959).

[3]James F. T. Bugenthal, ed., *Challenges of Humanistic Psychology* (New York: McGraw-Hill, 1967), p. vii.

[4]See A. G. Miller, ed., *The Social Psychology of Psychological Research* (New York: Free Press, 1972) for a representative treatment of methodological problems in experimental psychological research.

[5]*The Ghost in the Machine* is the title of a detailed (and acrid) critique of positivistic psychology by Arthur Koestler (New York: Macmillan, 1967).

[6]Herbert C. Kelman, "Human Use of Human Subjects: The Problem of Deception in Social Psychological Experiments,"*Psychological Bulletin* 67 (1967):1-11.

[7]David Bakan, "Psychology Can Now Kick the Science Habit," *Psychology Today* 5 (March 1972):26-28, 86-88.

[8]Earl R. Carlson and Rae Carlson, "Male and Female Subject in Personality Research," *Journal of Abnormal and Social Psychology* 61 (1960):482-83.

[9]See especially Donald T. Campbell and Julian C. Stanley, *Experimental and Quasi-Experimental Designs for Research* (Boston: Houghton Mifflin, 1966) for an acknowledged classic on the difficulties of producing truly generalizable results in psychology experiments; or Neil M. Agnew and Sandra W. Pike, *The Science Game*, 2d ed. (Englewood Cliffs, N.J.: Prentice-Hall, 1978), for a more elementary treatment.

[10]This particular set of field experiments was conducted by Irving M. Piliavin, Judith Rodin and Jane A. Piliavin. See their "Good Samaritanism: An Underground Phenomenon?" *Journal of Personality and Social Psychology* 13 (1969):289-99. For other examples of field experiments in psychology, see Leonard Bickman and Thomas Henchy, eds., *Beyond the Laboratory: Field Research in Social Psychology* (New York: McGraw-Hill, 1971).

[11]Henry W. Riecken, "Research Developments in the Social Sciences," in *Perspectives in Social Psychology*, ed. Otto Klineberg and Richard Christie (New York: Holt, Rinehart and Winston, 1965), p. 15.

[12]Arthur D. Schulman and Irwin Silverman, "Profile of Social Psychology: A Preliminary Application of 'Reference Analysis,' " *Journal of the History of the Behavioral Sciences* 8 (1972):232-36.

[13]Irwin Silverman, "Why Social Psychology Fails," *Canadian Psychological Review* 18 (1977):354.

[14]Bernard Berelson and Gary A. Steiner, *Human Behavior: An Inventory of Scientific Findings* (New York: Harcourt, Brace and World, 1964), p. 666.

[15]See C. Stephen Evans, *Preserving the Person: A Look at the Human Sciences* (Grand Rapids, Mich.: Baker Book House, 1982), p. 12. I have often wondered if this inconsistency which usually leads social scientists to be "better than their theories" is not one way in which God the Holy Spirit mercifully holds rampant evil in check.

[16]Summaries of experiments are adapted from Zick Rubin, "Jokers Wild in the Lab," *Psychology Today* 4 (December 1970):18-24; and Irwin Silverman, "Non-reactive Methods and the Law,"*American Psychologist* 38 (July 1975): 764-69. For more detailed information about each experiment, see (1) Dana

Bramel, "A Dissonance Theory Approach to Defensive Projection," *Journal of Abnormal and Social Psychology* 64 (1962):121-29; (2) J. Merrill Carlsmith and Alan E. Gross, "Some Effects of Guilt on Compliance," *Journal of Personality and Social Psychology* 11 (1969):232-39; (3) Elaine Walster, "The Effect of Self-Esteem on Romantic Liking," *Journal of Experimental Social Psychology* 6 (1967):371-80; and (4) Stanley Milgram, "A Behavioral Study of Obedience," *Journal of Abnormal and Social Psychology* 67 (1963):371-78.

[17]See Miller, *Social Psychology*, p. 75, and the rest of the volume for a representative sample of writings on the issue of ethics in experimentation.

[18]Julius Seeman, "Deception in Psychological Research," *American Psychologist* 24 (November 1969):1025-28; and Lawrence J. Stricker, "The True Deceiver," *Psychological Bulletin* 68 (1967):13-20.

[19]Diana Baumrind, "Some Thoughts on the Ethics of Research," *American Psychologist* 19 (June 1964):421.

[20]See McClintock, Spaulding and Turner, "Political Orientations."

[21]Indeed, such systematic debriefing after naturalistic experiments, even if it were possible, would gradually contribute both to subject sophsctication (leading persons in later experiments to react nonnaively) and to the boy-who-cried-wolf effect (i.e., the tendency to ignore any unusual event on the suspicion that it is "just another psychology experiment").

[22]Silverman, "Non-reactive Methods."

[23]American Psychological Association, *Casebook on Ethical Standards of Psychologists* (Washington, D.C.: American Psychological Association, 1967), and *Ethical Principles in the Conduct of Research with Human Participants* (Washington, D.C.: American Psychological Association, 1973).

[24]Robert Rosenthal, "Interpersonal Expectations: Effects of the Experimenter's Hypothesis," in *Artifact in Behavioral Research*, ed. Rosenthal and R. L. Rosnow (New York: Academic Press, 1969). See also Rosenthal, "The Pygmalion Effect Lives," *Psychology Today* 7 (September 1973):56-63.

[25]Robert Rosenthal, "Experimenter Attributes as Determinants of Subjects' Responses," *Journal of Projective Techniques and Personality Assessment* 27 (1963):324-31.

[26]See Rubin, "Jokers Wild."

[27]See, for example, Loren Baritz, *The Servants of Power: A History of the Use of the Social Sciences in American Industry* (New York: John Wiley, 1960); Steinar Kvale, "The Technological Paradigm of Psychological Research," *Journal of Phenomenological Psychology* 3 (1973):143-59; and Rolf Von Ekartsberg, "An Approach to Experiential Social Psychology," in *Duquesne Studies in Phenomenological Psychology*, vol. 1, ed. Amedeo Giorgi et al. (Pittsburgh: Duquesne University Press, 1973).

[28]Hugo Muensterberg, *Psychology and Industrial Efficiency* (New York: Houghton Mifflin, 1913), pp. 19-20.

[29]*The Life and Letters of Charles Darwin*, 3 vols., ed. Francis Darwin (London: John Murray, 1887), 1:81-82.

[30]David Bakan, *On Method: Towards a Reconstruction of Psychological In-*

vestigation (New York: Jossey-Bass, 1967), p. 48.

[31]Silverman, "Why Social Psychology Fails," pp. 356-57.

Chapter 3

[1]Thomas Kuhn, *The Structure of Scientific Revolutions*, 2d ed., The Internᴜ tional Encyclopedia of Unified Science, vol. 2, no. 2 (Chicago: University o Chicago Press, 1970). My own understanding of Kuhn and his significance for psychology was aided by Mary Vander Goot's "Paradigm Shifts: A Playful Application of Personal Construct Theory" (unpublished manuscript, Department of Psychology, Calvin College, Grand Rapids, Mich. 49506).

[2]Kuhn, *Scientific Revolutions*, p. viii.

[3]Ibid., pp. 90-91.

[4]Norman L. Munn, *Psychology* (Boston: Houghton Mifflin, 1966), p. 7; Clifford T. Morgan and Richard A. King, *Introduction to Psychology* (New York: McGraw-Hill, 1966), p. 4; Elton B. McNeil, *The Psychology of Being Human* (San Francisco: Canfield Press, 1974), p. 10; Robert E. Silverman, *Psychology* (Englewood Cliffs, N. J.: Prentice-Hall, 1974), p. 3.

[5]Ernest R. Hilgard, Richard L. Atkinson and Rita C. Atkinson, *Introduction to Psychology*, 7th ed. (New York: Harcourt, Brace, Jovanovich, 1979), p. 24.

[6]Paul L. Wachtel, "Investigation and Its Discontents: Some Constraints on Progress in Psychological Research," *American Psychologist* 35 (May 1980): 399-408.

[7]Kuhn, *Scientific Revolutions*, chapter 4.

[8]Evans, *Preserving the Person*, p. 69.

[9]Ibid., pp. 95-97.

[10]Chapter 5 of the Westminster Confession, quoted in Evans, *Preserving the Person*, p 99.

[11]Ibid., p. 100.

[12]Stanley L. Jaki, *Brain, Mind, and Computers* (South Bend, Ind.: Gateway Editions, 1969). Jaki's other works pertinent to the concerns of this chapter include *The Road of Science and the Ways to God* (Chicago: University of Chicago Press, 1978) and *The Origin of Science and the Science of Its Origin* (South Bend, Ind.: Regnery/Gateway, 1978).

[13]John C. Eccles, *Brain and Conscious Experience* (New York: Springer Verlag, 1966); Wilder Penfield, *The Mystery of the Mind* (Princeton, N.J.: Princeton University Press, 1975). See also P. Laslett, ed., *The Physical Basis of the Mind* (London: Macmillan & Co., 1950).

[14]Donald M. MacKay, *The Clockwork Image* (Downers Grove, Ill.: InterVarsity Press, 1974), p. 36. See also *his Human Science and Human Dignity* (Downers Grove, Ill.: InterVarsity Press, 1979) and Malcolm Jeeves, *Psychology and Christianity: The View Both Ways* (Downers Grove, Ill.: InterVarsity Press, 1976).

[15]MacKay, *Clockwork Image*, p. 37.

[16]Evans, *Preserving the Person*, pp. 88-91.

[17]See Michael Polanyi, *Personal Knowledge* (Chicago: University of Chicago

Press, 1958); Stephen Toulmin, *Foresight and Understanding* (Bloomington: Indiana University Press, 1961); and essays by Kuhn, Polanyi, Toulmin and Paul Feyerabend in *Criticism and the Growth of Knowledge*, ed. Imre Lakatos and Alan Musgrave (Cambridge: Cambridge University Press, 1970).

[18]MacKay, *Clockwork Image*, chapter 8. Evans, in his careful philosophical analysis of MacKay's position, concludes that MacKay's notion of freedom is so limited as to be only a slightly qualified determinism, and not freedom as required for either moral responsibility or a revised approach to doing human science. See *Preserving the Person*, chapter 9, especially pp. 108-17.

[19]MacKay, *Clockwork Image*, chapter 3, especially pp. 34-36.

[20]Evans, *Preserving the Person*, p. 110.

[21]See, for example, G. C. Berkouwer, *Man: The Image of God* (Grand Rapids, Mich.: Eerdmans, 1962); Hans W. Wolff, *Anthropology of the Old Testament* (Philadelphia: Fortress Press, 1974); and Wulstan Mork, *The Biblical Meaning of Man* (Milwaukee, Wis.: Bruce Publishing Co., 1967).

[22]George M. Marsden, *Fundamentalism and American Culture: The Shaping of Twentieth-Century Evangelicalism, 1870-1925* (New York: Oxford University Press, 1980), p. 55. See especially his chapter 6, "Dispensationalism and the Baconian Ideal."

[23]Theodore B. Bozeman, *Protestants in an Age of Science: The Baconian Ideal and Antebellum American Religious Thought* (Chapel Hill: University of North Carolina Press, 1977), especially pp. 30-31. Note that Scottish Common Sense Realism, because it was a British movement, had an effect on British nonconformist Christians as well. It is possible that both Jeeves and MacKay have inherited this legacy.

[24]Marsden, *Fundamentalism*, pp. 56-60.

[25]Ibid., p. 56.

[26]Ibid., pp. 58-59.

[27]I suspect that if this problem were overcome, the whole creation-evolution debate (for instance) among evangelicals in the natural sciences would be seen to be a red herring.

[28]Kenneth G. Elzinga, "A Christian View of Economic Order," *Reformed Journal* 31 (October 1981):13-16. My emphasis.

[29]Peter L. Benson and Merton P. Strommen, "Religion on Capitol Hill: How Beliefs Affect Voting in the U.S. Congress," *Psychology Today* 15 (December 1981):3, 46-57.

[30]Robert Nisbet, "Subjective Si! Objective No!" in Gresham Riley, ed., *Values, Objectivity and the Social Sciences* (Reading, Mass.: Addison-Wesley, 1974), pp. 19-20.

[31]See, for example, William J. McGuire, "The Yin and Yang of Progress in Social Psychology: Seven Koan," *Journal of Personality and Social Psychology* 26 (1973):446-51; Kenneth J. Gergen, "Towards Generative Theory," *Journal of Personality and Social Psychology* 36 (1978):1344-60; and Paul L. Wachtel, "Investigation and Its Discontents: Some Constraints on Progress in Psychological Research," *American Psychologist* 35 (May 1980):399-408.

[32]Serge Moscovici, "Society and Theory in Social Psychology," in *The Context of Social Psychology: A Critical Assessment*, ed. J. Israel and H. Tajfel (New York: Academic Press, 1972).

[33]In this I am in good company: see Gordon W. Allport's classic article, "The General and the Unique in Psychological Science," *Journal of Personality* 30 (1962):405-22, also reprinted in *Human Inquiry: A Sourcebook of New Paradigm Research*, ed. Peter Reason and John Rowan (New York: John Wiley & Sons, 1981).

[34]See, for example, Max Weber, *Theory of Economic and Social Organization* (New York: Oxford University Press, 1947); R. G. Collingwood, *The Idea of History* (Oxford: Clarendon Press, 1946) and *The Idea of a Science* (Oxford: Oxford University Press, 1944); and Peter Winch, *The Idea of a Social Science and Its Relation to Philosophy* (New York: Humanities Press, 1958).

[35]See particularly Reason and Rowan, *Human Inquiry*.

[36]Misiak and Sexton, *History of Psychology*, give a quite complete overview and bibliography of third-force psychology.

[37]See Giorgi, *Psychology as a Human Science;* Misiak and Sexton, *History of Psychology;* T. W. Wann, *Behaviorism and Phenomenology: Contrasting Bases for Modern Psychology* (Chicago: University of Chicago Press, 1964); and especially Ronald S. Valle and Mark King, *Existential-Phenomenological Alternatives for Psychology* (Oxford: Oxford University Press, 1978), for an orientation to existential and phenomenological movements in North American psychology.

[38]Erving Goffman, *Asylums*, (New York: Doubleday, 1961).

[39]See especially Carl R. Rogers, *Client-Centered Therapy: Its Current Practice, Implications and Theory* (Boston: Houghton Mifflin, 1951) and *On Becoming a Person* (Boston: Houghton Mifflin, 1961).

[40]For a thorough survey of methodological issues in cross-cultural psychology, see Harry C. Triandis, ed., *Handbook of Cross-Cultural Psychology* (Boston: Allyn and Bacon, 1980), especially vol. 1. The methodological debate in cross-cultural psychology (the *etic-emic* controversy) seems to have been temporarily settled by a compromise known as the *derived etic* approach, whereby the researcher brings his or her own theories, methods, etc., to the alien culture but is prepared to modify them in order to make them work "validly" (in the psychometric sense) in the new culture. Needless to say, this compromise is merely an adaptation of a basically positivistic approach and still leaves many cross-cultural researchers (including myself) uneasy.

[41]Paul Diesing, *Patterns of Discovery in the Social Sciences* (Chicago: Aldine-Atherton, 1971), pp. 137-38.

[42]See, for example, C. R. Jeffery and Ina A. Jeffery, "Psychosurgery and Behavior Modification," *American Behavioral Scientist* 18 (1975):685-722; Hilgard, Atkinson and Atkinson, *Introduction to Psychology*, chapter 15; C. S. Lewis, *The Abolition of Man* (London: Geoffrey Bles, 1941) and "The Humanitarian Theory of Punishment," in *God in the Dock* (Grand Rapids, Mich.: Eerdmans, 1970).

43Berkouwer, *Man*, p. 200.

44See especially Reason and Rowan, *Human Inquiry*, especially the article by Donald Bannister, "Personal Construct Theory and Research Method."

45Viktor Frankl, *Man's Search for Meaning* (New York: Simon & Schuster, 1962). I do not think that the uncovering of meaning as an end goal in psychological research requires a practical justification, even though it may have practical implications in the long run.

46Owen J. Flanagan, Jr., "Psychology, Progress and the Problem of Reflexivity: A Study in the Epistemological Foundations of Psychology," *Journal of the History of the Behavioral Sciences* 17 (1981):375-86.

47Currently there is one striking example of a human-science-oriented clinician's successfully exporting a theory and methodology to academic psychologists, namely, George A. Kelly, whose *Psychology of Personal Constructs* (New York: Norton, 1955) investigates human behavior on the premise that it is naively, yet rationally, scientific in character. Kelly's work has spawned a rich and continuing research tradition on both sides of the Atlantic.

48Evans, *Preserving the Person*, p. 131. For a more extended treatment of the intersubjectivity of experience, see Alfred Schutz, "Concept and Theory Formation in the Social Sciences," in his *Collected Papers*, ed. Maurice Natanson (The Hague: Martinus Nyhoff, 1962).

49Paul Ricoeur, *Freud and Philosophy: An Essay on Interpretation* (New Haven, Conn.: Yale University Press, 1970), pp. 30, 33. Ricoeur does not deal with positivism as an example of a "hermeneutic of suspicion." He deals primarily with Freud and incidentally with figures such as Marx and Nietzsche. However, I do not believe that I am distorting him in extending his analysis to include the positivistic tradition in psychology.

50Edmund Husserl, *The Idea of Phenomenology*, trans. William P. Aston and George Nahakian (The Hague: Martinus Nyhoff, 1964) and *Cartesian Meditations*, trans. Dorian Cairns (The Hague: Martinus Nyhoff, 1969); Joseph Kockelmans, *A First Introduction to Husserl's Phenomenology* (Pittsburgh: Duquesne University Press, 1967).

51Thomas Luckman, ed., *Phenomenology and Sociology* (Harmondsworth, U. K.: Penguin Books, 1978), p. 9.

52Giorgi, *Psychology as a Human Science*, especially chapter 2, "Investigation of Psychology Conceived as a Natural Science"; and Paul F. Colaizzi, "Psychological Research as the Phenomenologist Views It," in Valle and King, *Existential-Phenomenological Alternatives*, chapter 3.

53Allport, "The General and the Unique," p. 71.

54Steven W. Duck, *Personal Relations and Personal Constructs* (New York: John Wiley, 1973), especially chapters 3 and 6.

55The material in this section is drawn largely from Elizabeth Lines, "On Being Close Friends: A Phenomenological Analysis" (master's thesis, Department of Psychology, York University, Toronto, in preparation).

56For example, Valle and King, *Existential-Phenomenological Alternatives*, especially chapters 1-11; Reason and Rowan, *Human Inquiry*, especially chapters 11-21; Kelly, *Psychology of Personal Constructs;* Barney G. Glaser and Anselm L. Strauss, *The Discovery of Grounded Theory* (Chicago: Aldine, 1967); James F. T. Bugenthal, ed., *Challenges of Humanistic Psychology* (New York: McGraw-Hill, 1967); Shulamit Reinharz, *On Becoming a Social Scientist* (San Francisco: Jossey-Bass, 1979); E. Willems and H. Rausch, eds., *Naturalistic Viewpoints in Psychological Research* (New York: Holt, Rinehart and Winston, 1969); Diesing, *Patterns of Discovery.*

[57]Nicholas Wolterstorff, *Reason within the Bounds of Religion* (Grand Rapids, Mich.: Eerdman's, 1976), p. 14.

[58]Paul C. Vitz, *Psychology as Religion: The Cult of Self-Worship* (Grand Rapids, Mich.: Eerdman's, 1977), p. 62.

[59]Virginia L. Senders, in Michael Wertheimer et al., "Psychology and the Future," *American Psychologist* 33 (July 1978):631-46.

[60]The most prominent apologist for a transpersonal psychology is Charles Tart. See his *Altered States* (New York: John Wiley, 1969).

Index